SUBMARINERS
Real Life Stories From the Deep

SUBMARINERS

Real Life Stories From the Deep

All royalties from the sale of this book are being donated to the Submariners Memorial Fund and the Beatson Hospital, Glasgow

TEMPUS

The Submariners Memorial Fund

This fund is managed for the exclusive use of submariners, by the Royal Naval Benevolent Fund (RNBT). Any submariner past or present in need of assistance can make a claim against both these funds.

The Beatson Oncology Centre Fund

This unit is the leading non-surgical cancer treatment centre for the west of Scotland. It i not only involved in the treatment of patients, but also in carrying out clinical and laboratory research into possible new treatments and possible causes of cancer. Anything supported by the fund would not otherwise be supported by the NHS and is used to pay for patient care and comfort, and the training and education of staff within the centre.

First published 2006

Tempus Publishing Limited
The Mill, Brimscombe Port,
Stroud, Gloucestershire, GL5 2QG

© Keith Hall 2006

British Library Cataloguing in Publication Data.
A catalogue record for this book is available from the British Library.

ISBN 0 7524 2809 8

Typesetting and origination by Tempus Publishing Limited
Printed in Great Britain

Contents

Acknowledgements

Submariners' stories are not intended for an audience of one or, even worse, for the sterile ear of a tape recorder so I am particularly grateful to the following people for sharing their stories with me and allowing me to use them in this book: Pip Cox, Tony Smyth, Hugh Porter, Andy Lawrence, John Pounder, Mark Fuller, Allan McLelland, Jim McMaster, Tony Dance, Jim Drew, Barry Gibb, Derek Lilliman, Steve Bridge, Grant Maloney. I have purposely not credited them in the text, they will know who they are; hopefully the regulating staff won't.

I would like to thank the following organisations for permission to use their material and the waiving of their copyright fees.

AM Heath & Co. Ltd for permission to use extracts from Captain Compton-Halls book 'Submarines and the War at Sea 1914 to 18'.

Crown Copyright for all the MOD photographs.

Cdr Tall for permission to use the photographs from his book 'Submarines in Camera', written in conjunction with Peter Kemp.

I am also indebted to:

The 'Fleet Photographic Unit Clyde' for supplying the majority of the photographs and the stunning front cover.

Ellen Milgrew for typing the bulk of the manuscript. Ken Collins for allowing me to use the 'Submariners Bond'.

Captain P. Walker Royal Navy (captain of the Faslane flotilla) for writing the foreword.

And Tempus Publishing for the opportunity to state and prove the case.

Finally, I ask for forgiveness from any contributors who may have been unintentionally omitted from these acknowledgements.

Foreword

I felt very honoured when Keith Hall asked me to write this foreword for his latest book, but was surprised when he revealed the subject matter. A collection of submariners' dits (or anecdotes to the uninitiated), appeared to be a significant departure from the local history that has characterised his earlier, beautifully researched volumes. However, I quickly came to the conclusion that this was not really the case because such stories are a fundamental part of the history of our beloved submarine service; and we all recognise that it is churlish to allow strict observance of the absolute facts to get in the way of a good story!

These dits will strike a chord with all submariners, both serving and retired, but will only scratch the surface of a rich seam of stories that exists out there. Perhaps this book will lead to a sequel or two: I do hope so. It is also worthy of note that, as with his previous books, Keith Hall is donating all royalties to worthy causes, thus demonstrating that other, often unsung, trait of the submariner – generosity.

I could not conclude the foreword to such a book without contributing a story of my own and I can confirm that this is fact and not fiction! So here goes…

In the autumn of 1972, I was the Torpedo Officer of HMS Rorqual and we were taking part in a large NATO exercise up in the Norwegian Sea. Unfortunately, we suffered a succession of defects in short order, losing first the port diesel generator and then the starboard. With a rapidly depleting battery, a frigate was detached to stand by us and provide additional support including hot meals flown across by its Wasp helicopter. After some thirty-six hours, one generator was restored and we limped into Ramsfjordnes, the northern outpost of the Norwegian Navy, to fix the other. Accommodation ashore was rudimentary but very welcome after the unventilated conditions on-board and the knackered members of the ME Department were in better spirits the next morning. Having been on duty myself and staying on-board, I enquired of the SPO (stoker petty officer), a larger than life Cockney, how his first full night's sleep for several days had been. 'Aw right sir' he said 'but it took me half an hour to unpick me sleepin' bag that some bleedin' stupid Norwegian had stitched up.' This was clearly SPO's first encounter with a duvet but I didn't have the heart to tell him then! However, it illustrates quite well the fact that submariners are traditionally creatures of habit and are deeply suspicious of innovation.

Read on and enjoy.

Captain Pat Walker Royal Navy
Captain Faslane Flotilla
August 2005

Introduction

In a book about HMS *Dolphin*, the submariners' spiritual home, I referred to the submariner as the 'thinking man's matelot'. The publisher has invited me to defend and explain this seemingly extravagant and surreal claim.

What makes the submariner so special? His renowned bravery really needs no further comment; nor do his stamina, intelligence, charm, devotion to duty and commitment to the service (a fact borne out by my service records, which over the years have failed to mention my stamina, intelligence, etc.). The mental tutoring the submariner receives in his formative years undoubtedly leaves its mark. The 'been there, seen it, done it' mentality ensures that wherever a submariner's head may finish up, his feet are always firmly on the ground.

Daisy Adams (page 13) and the young man from D2 (Page 14) are members of every submarine ship's company and every Submarine Association branch. They are men that don't belong in a world of performance indicators or productivity targets; they are men that are made not to be managed, but led and this, in part, helps to explain the close-knit, self-reliant community that is a submarine crew. It is a brotherhood that spans nations and generations; submariners are submariners the world over, and submariners are submariners regardless of when they served. While the language might change, and the once young bodies tend to mature, the ethos and the stories they give rise too, remain the same.

The submariners unique qualities can, perhaps, be best illustrated with the following, beyond all shadow of a doubt, true story:

During the Second World War a British submarine, operating in the Mediterranean, came under heavy depth charge attack. The chief stoker was mortally wounded during the attack. He fell to the control room deck, blood pouring from a gaping head wound.

'Is that you SPO?' mumbled the chief.

'Yes chief' replied the shocked SPO, cradling the injured chief stoker in his arms.

'Is Stoker Grimshaw here?'

'Yes chief' cried Grimshaw as another depth charge exploded close to the port side.

'…and young MEM (Marine Engineering Mechanic) Smith, is he with me?' whispered the chief stoker.

'Yes chief' whimpered the young MEM, wiping a tear from his bloodshot eye, 'Yes chief, I'm here.'

'SPO, Grimshaw, Smith' gasped the chief stoker, mustering all his rapidly failing strength, 'then who the **** is on the panel?!'

It is not uncommon in the armed services, to claim that one regiment is better than another; one ship's company is superior to another ship's, even one country's services are better than another's. It is this unsolicited and unofficial rivalry that, in part, makes the British service-man the best in the world. The only difference is that when a submariner says he's the best, he is speaking from the enviable position of truth. It is worth repeating that the submariner, this human Turner Prize, is the chosen keeper of the 'holy grail' of all sea-going parables, the legendary 'Revolving Bar' dit.

Keith Hall
Tumbledown Cottage

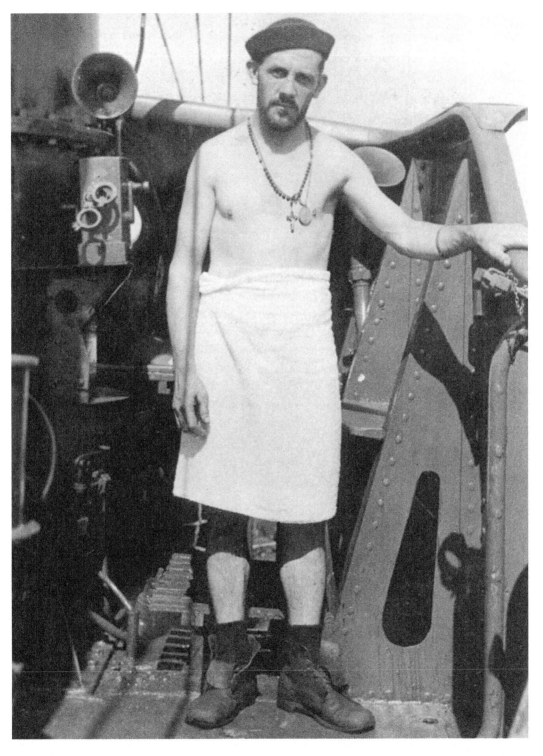

AB Daisy Adams in 'tropical rig', on HMS Orpheus during the 1930s, obviously making an effort to look his best for the camera.

Left: Casual and comfortable. A member of D2's ship company looking interesting and windswept.

Below: C-boats leaving harbour.

one

Underhand, underwater – and damned un-English

It was not just that submarines and their crews did not fit into the class-ridden Edwardian Navy; there was also a fear that if submarines were accepted, they would render the stupendous British fleet obsolete (they would be cheaper and would require less crew) and it is hard to see the prestige of serving in a 50ft semi-submerged steel tube. That submarines were 'considered the weapon of a weaker nation' was just one of the arguments offered to preserve the primacy of the colossal surface fleet. Another tack to win the argument was to lay claim to the moral high ground; Admiral Cherry was of the opinion that all submariners should be 'hung as pirates'. So the first submarines were obtained in order to merely assess them and, if truth be told, probably because the 'old enemy' France had them.

That said, the fledgling submarine service did little to endear itself to the Navy at large. The polished quarterdecks of the class-ridden surface fleet were not for submariners and conversely the smelly new-fangled craft crewed by 'unwashed chauffeurs' were not at all to the liking of the 'gentlemen' of the established Navy. The fact that gentlemen never dirtied their hands with a trade might account for the submariner's nickname for his particular calling.

★ ★ ★

The beloved sea riders had been working up a submarine for several very long days, and hard though it is to believe, they had given the crew a particularly hard time. Just before they left they asked the chef if he could make them up some sandwiches for the rail journey when they left the submarine the next morning. The chef duly obliged and presented the off-going sea riders with a large brown paper bag just before they were transferred by boat to shore. A few hours into the rail journey they opened their 'bag meal'. Just as the chef had promised, the bag was full of sandwiches. They got themselves a few 'tinnies' and settled down for a well-deserved lunch. They bit into the sandwiches only to discover that in-between the two slices of bread were neatly cut squares of cardboard, with 'for exercise ham; for exercise cheese and onion' written on them.

★ ★ ★

Many years ago when this chappie was young and good looking (now I am youngish but still good looking), I was bravely struggling to complete my part three training and we were ever so lucky to have some of those wonderful kind and caring sea riders down to assist with our index etc, 'Will all part threes muster in the fore ends' was piped. We had a charming and compassionate sea rider to instruct us in the mysteries of the oxygen generator and the Dos and Don'ts of using the candles. At the end of a very instructive half-hour lecture I was invited to open up and check a candle before burning. I, being quite a shy part three, very diffidently pointed out 'Staff, this candle smells a bit of diesel'. 'Give it here son' he said, 'I'll cast my expert eye over it.'

Well, after telling me in no uncertain terms that there was nothing wrong with the candle and that I should grow up and learn about life in a blue suit, he loaded the candle into the generator. When the .22 cartridge ignited it took about twelve seconds for this horrible whooshing sound and many pretty coloured sparks to come belching out of the oxygen generator. Not to put too fine a point to it but the sea rider was climbing over part threes'

Keeping a weathered eye.

Torpedo compartment – then. The four bow tubes on an early submarine.

Torpedo compartment – now.

backs to get out the fore ends. It ended up with a couple of us novice part threes shutting down the bulkhead just before the oxygen generator exploded. After surfacing to clear smoke and deal with the few small fires that had started in the compartment, we rather naively thought that the sea rider might just come back to us to apologise for his actions. Glad we didn't hold our breath. But at least if nothing else, we realised that even the mighty screw up badly.

★　★　★

Submarine alongside at Devonport during CSST (Captain Sea Shore Training) inspection:

Inspecting officer: 'Chief doc, where would you take your first reading in the event of a reactor core meltdown?'

CPOMA: 'Preston sir!'

Inspecting officer: 'Don't be stupid chief.'

CPOMA: 'Who's being stupid sir?'

★　★　★

A CSST officer for some reason finished every question with 'Batman'. He asked the console operator: 'Why have we got two ballast pumps Batman?'

System console operator: 'One for me and one for Robin sir!'

★　★　★

Phased pay awards were not very popular when introduced a few years ago. An admiral, who was deeply involved in the introduction, was the VIP on a T-boat returning from patrol. As is the custom on these occasions, the admiral visited the senior rates mess. When asked, by the mess pres if he would like a drink, he asked for a CSB. The mess pres handed him half a glass of beer in a pint glass.

'Oh' said the admiral, 'short measure chief'.

'Oh no sir, fifty per cent now, fifty per cent in October!'

★　★　★

In the halcyon days before CSST, FOSM and his staff used to conduct the work ups. During a man overboard exercise on HMS *Dreadnought* the chief doc, who was on the casing, failed to notice that the recovered 'victim was being lowered down the access hatch, head first, in the Neil Robertson stretcher'. FOSM leaned over the fin,

'What's going on chief? He's upside down!'

The chief doc looked round and to his horror saw the rescued man's boots just disappearing down the hatch.

'It's to get the water out of his lungs sir, immersion victim!' replied the quick-thinking medic.

'Oh very good doc'. Two weeks later FOSM failed an O-boat for getting the drill right.

…and while on the subject of *Dreadnought's* stretcher…

The Neil Robertson stretcher was stowed in a cupboard in the SR's (senior rate's) mess. To save time and show what switched-on kiddies the medics were, all sorts of medical bits and pieces were tied on, with string, to the stretcher. In an emergency all you had to do was grab the Neil Robertson and run to the scene and you'd front-up better equipped than your average ambulance. During work up, the chief doc knew that the next exercise would involve an injured man in the control room. At the first press of the klaxon, the chief doc reached into the cupboard, grabbed his kit and raced to the control room. He got to the control room just as the officer of the day was finishing the pipe.

D-class submarines in Torquay.

'Good God chief doc,' he said in amazement, 'very impressive but what are you doing with the ironing board under your arm?!'

★ ★ ★

Hard though it is to believe, a submariner from HMS *Dreadnought* sneaked into the ambassador's party in Gibraltar.

'...and what do you do?' the gatecrasher was asked.

'Oh I travel in metal tubes for the British government'.

★ ★ ★

SCENE: *CPO's dining hall, HMS* Dolphin.

Admiral walking round during midday meal and stops at a table of old and bold chiefs...

Admiral: 'Why are you not eating the peas chief?'

Chief: 'They're tough sir.'

The admiral lifts an unused fork from the centre of the table, selects a pea from the chief's plate and eats it ...

Admiral: 'This one is fine chief, very soft indeed.'

Chief: 'It should be sir; I've been chewing it for twenty minutes.'

Weight Conscious Stoker

On watch, one middle watch in the donk shop of the *Sealion*, to the watch-keeper's surprise, a figure appeared from aft in a fear nought suit. Much to our surprise he stopped in the centre (between the crankcases of two diesel engines – gap of about a foot) where it gets very hot, (when working up in the winter, a good few members of the crew would stand here for the warmth.)

It turned out he was using the place as a sauna to sweat out a few calories. Unfortunately, he fainted and had to be carried back to the mess.

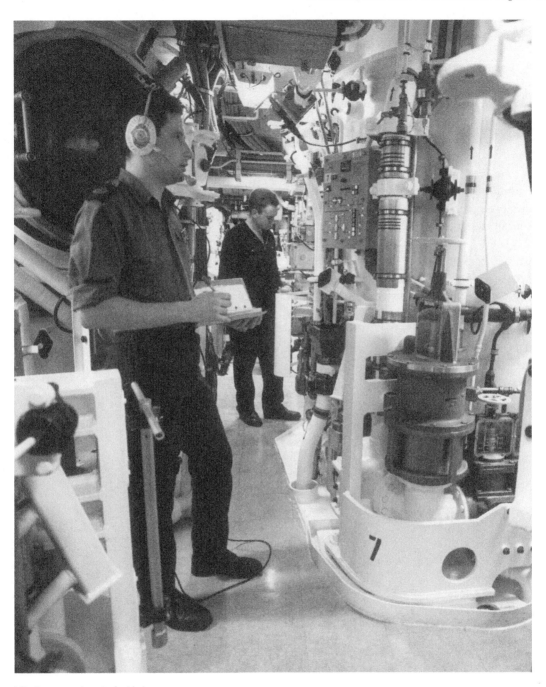

Missile compartment of a V-class.

Shining Lights

A young, fresh, out-of-the-box LWEA in *Dolphin* was seen shining a torch around the jetty. When asked what he was doing he said he'd been told to 'charge up the yellow lines'.

★　★　★

During a fire exercise on work-up on *Revenge*, the captain (Richard Wraith) was in the control room. Unusually, he did not have a cigarette in his mouth (this is the captain who, if he was out of fags would take fifty per cent of the fags the nearest rating had, but would also take the cardboard packet, leaving the donor with a fist full of fags and nowhere to put them) as he was wearing, like the rest of the control room watch-keepers, his EBS (emergency breathing system) mask. The XO (executive officer – whose name I can't remember, but hopefully he still can) was also in the control room, but decided he had to go to DCHQ. He therefore unplugged his EBS mask and fleeted out. Or so he thought. He was quickly stopped, with his head snapping backwards, by the hose of his EBS, which was still plugged in. Meanwhile, the captain was going a funny grey-blue colour due to the fact that a certain XO had unplugged him from the EBS coupling and was trying to run off with his EBS hose.

It was during the same exercise that the SCO (signal communications officer) was on the periscope whilst wearing his EBS. (The SCO was such a right-winger he made Paul Turnbull look like a liberal.) He almost managed to strangle himself with the hose of his EBS mask as he kept going round the same way using the periscope's torque assist, instead of going one way and then the other.

two

Should be hung as pirates...

Admiral Wilson and probably all submarine captains at one time or another

The individualistic lifestyle and unorthodox dress sense of the submariner has led to frequent misunderstandings with members of the Regulating Branch. These disagreements are not entirely the fault of the misunderstood submariner, one only has to think of the regulators waiting to pounce on submariners as they returned from patrol at the tunnel at Faslane to realise that the submariner is an unfortunate, hapless misunderstood soul. In all fairness the situation was not helped when a submariner walked into the regulating office at Faslane and looked at the display board that had the pictures of ratings that had deserted. 'Oh' he said to a nearby leading regulator, 'Why didn't you keep hold of them when you took the pictures?'

★ ★ ★

There is a story about a leading regulator being 'kidnapped' and taken on patrol to show him what conditions submariners have to put up with. Entertaining though the story is I am not sure if it is true, I've heard that it was a *Dolphin* boat, then an SM2 boat and finally a Faslane boat, and whilst not wishing to question the integrity of a submariner's story – I just cannot see one reggie doing that amount of sea time.

That aside, it still came as a great surprise, when I started compiling this book just how quickly this section filled up.

A CPO, accompanied by his trusty PO, walked into the regulating office in Alecto Colonnade. There were two leading regulators in the office.

'Okay' said the chief 'which one of you is reading and which one is writing?' It should be mentioned that the incident took place in the late afternoon.

'I think chief, that you should go away for a while', boomed the master at arms from his office somewhere in the depths of the regulating office. The chief and the PO left, only to reappear a short time later,

'Alright' said the chief, 'you've had ten minutes, now which round is it?'

A Charitable Rogue

On an early S-boat in build, I was the coxswain's dog, doing all the day-to-day administration which the coxswain signed at the end of the day. There were not too many sailors in the group at the time and the build had only just started. Work for me was steady but not frantic. For the coxswain it was less stressful, I seem to remember seeing him briefly in the morning and then quite late in the afternoon just before secure. His whereabouts in between were taken up visiting all the landlords and landladies of the accommodated sailors, and funny old thing, they were mostly in public houses!

The coxswain I will call Peter Rogue, for that will be enough to let everyone know who he is. He was a genuinely charitable chap, but his methods were sometimes questionable. Like the time the Sea Cadets gained a Bosun dinghy at the same time the building group lost one. He was also an avid fundraiser for worthy causes and really worked quite hard to help local charities and societies. He was especially fond of the local Sea Cadet unit. One day he decided we would have a barbeque – a large one. All the ship's company would go and would bring guests, tickets were well priced and entertainment would also be provided. It was to take place on a piece of common land on Walney Island. The ship's company rallied around making the grills, ordering the food, arranging transport and getting a couple of marquees from the local TA unit. The event went off very well indeed and even raised some money for charity, everyone was happy.

Some months later our stores team joined the group, and within just a few days the POSA (petty officer stores assistant) wanted to see the coxswain. Not an easy task that. However, I tracked down the coxswain and made arrangements for the POSA to meet him in the office the following afternoon. Next afternoon the POSA arrived, no coxswain. The POSA left after a very considerable wait. The POSA tried several times to contact or meet with the coxswain but Peter was as elusive as the scarlet pimpernel. It soon became clear that the coxswain didn't want to meet the POSA. Some weeks later, after some careful stalking, the POSA caught up with the coxswain in the office late in the afternoon.

The discussion concerned a couple of marquees belonging to the Territorial Army that had not been returned. It transpired that the coxswain had 'given' the marquees to a very deserving organization and couldn't possibly give them back. The coxswain and the POSA were old friends and thought about the problem for a little while. The POSA turned to me and said, 'you are a sailor aren't you?' to which I replied 'yes'. He asked me to go to the rigging shop, get a piece of green canvas, have a brass eye sewn into it and then splice a short length of green rope through the eye. He then asked me to get a short length of wooden pole about 2ft long and using an axe, damage both ends then paint it green. I was curious, but did as I was told.

The following day I went to the stores with the acquired items and looked on entirely bemused as the POSA produced a blowtorch and proceeded to scorch the poles and canvas.

He explained that he would return these things to the army, saying that during the barbeque the marquees had caught fire and no longer existed. Such is the store's system that it was believed and no further action was required.

★ ★ ★

A rather amusing thing happened when I did my coxswain's course in 1957 at HMS *Excellent*, Whale Island. There were only two on the course, a bloke named 'Daisy' Adams and myself. We had to live in *Pompey* RNB as there was no room in *Excellent*. Both of us having bicycles, we pedalled each day from RNB through North End to Whale Island and because we were on course we wore boots and gaiters. Every day we rode past the quartermasters' staff at the main gate, over the island to the far side where the regulating school was and nobody said a word to us! On the last day of the course we only had to go to the school to get our examination results so we didn't bother to wear our boots and gaiters. In consequence we were stopped at the main gate to produce ID, stopped on the parade ground by a chief GI who wanted to know who we were and hollered at by some lieutenant wearing patent leather gaiters who we chose to ignore, nipping down the steps to the regulating school! It is amazing what a pair of boots and gaiters can do for you. I think it is called 'gait and gaiters mentality'?

★ ★ ★

In 1958 while I was the coxswain of the *Tabard* we visited Tripoli in North Africa, (before Gadaffi's time). The British Army invited us out to their camp in the desert for a sporty/pissy weekend. Being the cox', I was taken under the wing of the regimental sergeant major of some Welsh regiment. Apparently he was a bit of a tarter as nobody could speak to him without springing to attention and shouting 'sah!' at the top of their voice. After a while this began to get through to me, especially after dinner and speeches when every WO and Sgt in the mess insisted on coming over and with the words 'Sah' at the top of their voice and insisting on buying us a drink.

As you can imagine when I retired to my room I was pretty full and ready for a good night's sleep. Imagine my surprise when at six o'clock in the morning I was awakened by a pounding on the door. Tottering out of bed with a mouth like the bottom of a baby's pram (all s*** and biscuit crumbs) I opened the door to be confronted by a 6ft 6in very irate duty sergeant with an axe helve under his right arm. His military style moustache was bristling and steam was literally coming out of his ears. He greeted me with the words

'Sah, I have just been to shake your men as it is *reveille* and they have told me in no uncertain terms to F*** O**', (one word rhymed with luck and one with cough!) 'will you come and sort them out, sah?'

My answer to this was that if I went anywhere near them at this time on a Sunday morning I would get told exactly the same and I had no intention of going anywhere near them until a civilised hour.

I really do not think that the sergeant was very impressed with discipline in the Royal Navy that day!

The Tale of The Inveraray Raiders

1980 was a good year for HMS/M *Spartan*. The newest boat in the fleet had just completed work-up and was carrying out trials in the northern fleet exercise areas in the first part of the year. The crew, full of pride and team spirit was willing to do anything to prove its

worth. The country was fascinated by the SAS as the Iranian Embassy siege had recently happened in London. On-board, our film library contained great films like *Smokie and the Bandit*, *WW and the Dixie Dance Kings* and of course *The Raid on Entebbe*, the fateful mission of a daring hostage snatched by the Israelis.

The boat had cruised through work-up with ease and the crew had gelled into a team, many of the friendships made then (over twenty-five years ago) have still lasting to this day. The cox'n, Harry Harrison, a legend in his own lifetime, had arranged a coach trip (run ashore) to test the new all-day opening hours in Scotland, and as I at the time had just completed my part three and had recently been promoted to LMEM, was selected by my chief stoker, Dave George, to go on the run and was instructed to muster in civvies by the quartermaster's lobby at half-past nine the next morning with about thirty others.

A pusser's coach arrived, 'Royal Navy' emblazoned down the side, we all jumped on not knowing what to expect and before we had reached Garelochead a case of beer was open and evaporated, (well it disappeared somewhere!) We arrived in Inveraray just before opening time. The ten minutes were spent looking at the various highland gift and wool shops, one of which had a good-looking female mannequin dummy standing outside wearing a kilt and cashmere wool sweater, looking very attractive. A couple of beers in the George and later, and as we were about to embark the coach for our next port of call, boy-o-boy did she look even more attractive. There was something that said to us that she was being held against her will and that she needed a good run ashore to cheer her up.

I remember saying something like 'come on, let's kidnap that dummy for the rest of the day' and before I knew it, leading seamen 'Ginge' Neil Geoghan and myself were running across the street, in stealth as befitting

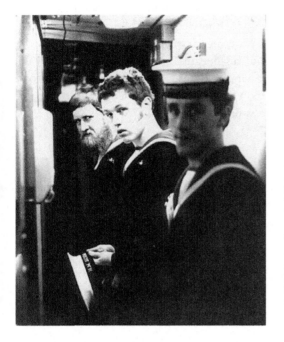

TO OPERATE W.C. DISCHARGE.

1. CHARGE AIR BOTTLE AND OPEN SEA AND N.R. VAL
2. OPEN FLUSH INLET VALVE WITH CARE.
3. FREE LEVER AND BRING TO PAUSE.
4. BRING LEVER TO FLUSHING.
5. BRING LEVER TO DISCHARGE.
6. BRING LEVER TO PAUSE.
   RETURN LEVER TO NORMAL AND LOCK.
9. CLOSE ALL VALVES.

Above left: The Inveraray raiders

Above right: How to flush!

of the silent service to mount our raid. The lads on the bus watched and cheered as we upended the hostage and started running back to the bus. It must have been quite a sight. I now know that mannequins top and bottom are held together by a spigot pin and gravity. If the person at the front runs faster than the one behind, it looks as though the body is getting longer. Other coach-trippers and the blue rinse brigade were shocked at the sight of the girl they thought we were carrying being stretched and then ripped apart by our valiant efforts to free her of her boring life.

The rest of the afternoon saw her accompany us to bars, pose in various states of dress belonging to others in the party (who were also in various states of dress or hers!), have beer spilt on her etc... During the later part of the day we decided to take her back. So, very

worse for wear, we dropped her back to the shop in a very dishevelled state but I am sure there was a smile on her face and a twinkle in her eye. Unfortunately one of her hands was missing but was later found on the floor of the bus. Harry, the coxswain, kept it and when the Jimmy (Lt CDR Dan Connelly) asked him if there was a spare hand available, his answer was always 'Here you are, sir!'

The run was a great success and the dits went on until well after we had sailed.

Then the signal came in. The shop had contacted the base to ask who was using the Royal Navy coach and that the dummy had been liberated for part of the day. The discipline office had got hold of this information and took it to read hang the guilty b******'s. The owner of the shop wanted compensation for the jumper that had been stretched, (probably due to an amorous groper!) plus did we have the missing hand? That we couldn't deny. Every officer on-board had by now fallen for Harry's joke and as soon as we hit Faslane, MOD CID (plain-clothed MOD police) were down to ask questions. A whip round paid for the damage, chocolates and flowers for the shop and they seemed very satisfied with the outcome, treating it all with good humour. Ginge and myself owned up like the mugs we were and the rest stayed stum. The heros of Inveraray were now the outcasts and after the third degree from the CID and a great bollocking from the CO, CDR Nigel Goodwin, we ended up with a £40 fine. Considering we were only on £120 a month that was a sore hole in the pocket!

Yet Another True Story

Whilst serving on the *Seascout* in 1952 as a young AB (able seaman) we took a very tall Major Farquharson of the army to sea with us for a three-day exercise.

One day whilst on the surface I was look-out during the eight to eleven watch when the message came up the voice pipe

'Permission for the major to come on the bridge for fresh air'. This was granted, of course and up came the major.

Fifteen minutes later I was due to be relieved and the message came:

'Permission to relieve look-out'.

'Very good' was the reply.

Up came my relief, who had obviously forgotten that the major was on the bridge and half-way out of the upper hatch saw this body leaning over the bridge. Thinking it was me, he rammed his index finger in a place on the human body that never sees daylight (i.e. Ducker's) with the words 'Wotcha, bash!'

The indignant and horrified major raised himself to his full 6ft 6in and said

'I am Major Farqhuarson of the Black Watch', to which my relief, quick as a flash, said

'Leading Seaman Cotnam, Green Watch!' and disappeared back down the hatch again, leaving me to do another spell as look-out. He wouldn't come back up while the major was on the bridge.

★ ★ ★

An officer came on-board over the forward brow with his grip in one hand and his numbers one and two on a hanger in the other. Halfway over the brow he attempted to throw the hanger over his shoulder. However, the hanger broke and both sets of uniform landed in the drink. The trot sentry, quick as a flash, made the following main broadcast:

'Safeguard, safeguard, officers laggin' in the oggin, duty diver to the casing at the rush.'

He got three days stoppage of leave for it.

★ ★ ★

With guests on-board the submarine on one occasion, the officer of the day asked the lower deck trot to pipe

'Heads and bathrooms are out of action until further notice'.

The lower deck trot piped 'Heads and bathrooms out of action. Stop shitting, stop shitting, stop shitting…'

He got fourteen days stoppage of leave.

★ ★ ★

My twenty-first birthday is worth a short mention! On our arrival in Singapore we were put into dry dock to have a bottom scrape and whilst in there my birthday, 18 January, came around. In those days the Royal Navy issued an eighth of a pint to each lower deck rating at approximately eleven o'clock each day. At this time, just after the Second World War we were issued 'one and one' as opposed to 'two and one' as decreed by my Lords Commissioners of the Admiralty.

It being my birthday, apart from my own tot I partook of 'sippers' or 'gulpers' from about everybody in the seaman's mess and then next door in the stoker's mess!

The next thing I remember was coming to in the bottom of the dry dock at half past two the following morning. I spent the following day very hung-over and with not a clue of what I had done the day before on my twenty-first birthday!!

★ ★ ★

After leaving Australia in 1966 having come to the end of my stay as the Escape Cox'n for the 4th S/M Division, I was told I had a draft to the Polaris Submarine *Renown,* then being built at Birkenhead. Whilst on my foreign leave I received a telegram to contact the drafting office in *Dolphin.*

Phoning them I found out my draft had been changed to the *Repulse* at Barrow but the biggest surprise was to be told to report the following Monday to HMS *Excellent* to do an MAA's (master at arms') course!

It appears that somebody in the bureaucratic hierarchy had the brilliant idea that coxswains drafted to Polaris boats should be a qualified MAA!

Having just returned from Australia I had very little in the way of uniform kit, most of it coming home by sea, so I reported on the Monday morning in my only blue suit (with gold badges). Lt Reg D'earth was in charge of the school and MAA Ribbons was the instructor, all the rest of the class including 'Happy' Day (deceased) and the RPOs were in red badges, which didn't go down very well. Neither were they pleased when I informed them that my boots, (so that I could wear 'boots and gaiters' whilst on the course) were in my kit bag somewhere between Australia

and England. I failed to mention that I did not possess a pair of boots – anyway, whoever heard of a coxswain of nine years standing owning a pair of boots!

As you can imagine this was not a very auspicious start to my course but I looked at the rest of the class and thought to myself, 'This lot is not going to beat me, especially the RPOs'. And with a lot of boning on my part, I came second in the class. The only RPO to beat me was an SD candidate named Bishop who I met out here in Australia many years later as a LCDR Reg RAN.

'Happy' Day I am sorry to say found it a bit of a struggle and till the day he died I don't believe he could tell the difference between 'repeated' and 'aggravated leave breaking'!

It is my belief that at the time, the regulating school were not too happy at coxswains doing this course, not even admitting that we were qualified MAAs, only saying that we had completed an 'Extended Regulating Course'.

★ ★ ★

SCENE: P&O S/M alongside during DED.
Wrecker coming on-board adrift…

OOD: 'You're three hours adrift wrecker, you can stand by for big wacks from the skipper.'

Wrecker: 'Sorry sir, me dad got burned this morning…'

OOD: 'Good God wrecker, burned badly????'

Wrecker: 'They don't mess about at the crematorium…'

Another True Story?

This happened on-board HMS/M *Token* tied up (secured, if you are ward room!) to the jetty at HMS *Dolphin.*

The trot sentry was a stoker, he came from the West Country somewhere in Cornwall so his name was Jan. Jan was a good bloke, a great 'oppo' for a run ashore, always ready for a joke but his ambition always was to have a shot at the ward room. If he could put one over the officers it would make his day. He never tried anything that would endanger anyone and sometimes the officers never even knew they had been had.

On-board *Token* we had an engineer officer who was one of those people who, when dressed in a suit, always looked as if the suit was trying to get away from him. The shirt, which five minutes before would have been crisp, would suddenly become wrinkled, the tie would creep around the neck, the trousers would start to hang down and the shirt tail would hang half in and half out of the pants, (*a right bloody scram bag!*). In white overalls he looked the perfect officer but in a suit, no chance!

This was the time when only officers were allowed ashore in 'Mufti' (civilian clothing). The lower deck still had to wear uniform ashore.

The 'civvies' that the engineer officer wore didn't enhance his appearance either. He appeared on the casing in a pair of sagging corduroy trousers, a jumper three sizes too big with leather patches on the elbows to stop his elbows showing through and a crumpled shirt. He proceeded over the gangplank and headed for the *Dolphin* main gate leaving Jan shaking his head after the apparition he had just seen.

Half an hour later the first lieutenant (Jimmy) came along the jetty and stopped at the gangplank but didn't cross it and sang out to Jan.

'Trot sentry, is the engineer on-board?'

Jan answered, 'No sir, he's gone ashore fishing'

This puzzled the Jimmy who half to himself and half to Jan said, 'I didn't think he was interested in fishing!' To this, Jan replied 'Well

sir, by the clothes he is wearing he wouldn't be going anywhere else'. Now thoroughly confused, the Jimmy could only stare at Jan and finding no further help forthcoming turned on his heels and walked away, leaving Jan well pleased with his latest tilt at the ward room and anxious for his relief so that he could tell the rest of the duty watch all about it!

Next day whilst 'turned too' in the engine room with a tin of Bluebell in one hand and a wad of cotton waste in the other, Jan was busily polishing the bright-work when the chief stoker informed him that the engineer officer required him in the control room with his cap. Now everybody knew the engineer officer would never put anybody in the 'Rattle' so they crept forward to see what was going on. There, Jan was being given a right rollicking. Jan was leaning back on his heels the engineer officer about 6in from his face wagging his index finger about an inch from Jan's nose.

When Jan came back into the 'donk shop', still wearing his insuppressible grin, and was asked what had happened, he remarked that the engineer wanted Jan to take him ashore to buy some decent gear from Greenburghs then disappears to the token's mess-deck inboard.

The chief stoker told us what really happened. The engineer said that if Jan didn't stop being the 'smart-arse' he would find himself in Chatham Barracks on the D/B (Double Bottom Bilges) cleaning party for the rest of his time in the Royal Navy. He went on to say that as he knew so much about dress, he ought to get himself inboard where he would find the 'jaunty' (MAA) from the *Dolphin* regulating office waiting to give him a kit muster.

This was indeed a master stroke by the engineer, the regulating staff as well as the 'jaunty' were General Service and didn't think much of submariners who thought they were better than anybody else and thought they could wander around *Dolphin* in their own 'rig of

The joining booklet for the Third Submarine Squadron. This section probably explains why this chapter is the largest in the book.

Special Week-end Coaches. The Regulating Office, H.M.S. ADAMANT, arranges special coaches to any destination if the numbers requiring the facilities are sufficient.

Local Buses. (SEE TIME-TABLE ON BACK PAGES.)

Taxicabs. Robertsons (*Tel.*: Helensburgh 1135)
Blacks (*Tel.*: Helensburgh 1238)

Note: The return trip is charged for Helensburgh even though you go only one way. Cost 15s.

Clubs

The Squadron Club, Faslane. For Leading ratings and below. Bar, Lounge, Snacks, Billiard Tables.

Bar opening times: Week-days	1800–2200
Saturdays	1200–1330
	1800–2200
Sundays	1200–1330
	1900–2200

The Club closes half an hour after the bar.

Vista, Faslane. The Senior Ratings Club for C.P.O.'s and P.O.'s Bar, Lounge and Snacks.

Bar opening times: Week-days	1800–2230
Saturdays	1200–1400 and
and Sundays	1900–2230

The Club closes at 2300 on week-days and 1500 and 2300 on Saturdays and Sundays.

Atlantic House and Pacific House, York St, Glasgow. Bed only at 5s. and 7s. 6d. (*Tel.*: Central 4916).

Church of Scotland Hostel, Helensburgh. This Hostel is in the buildings of the Old Parish Church (by the clock tower at the foot of Sinclair St.). There are 38 beds in single cubicles, games rooms, a quiet room, showers and lockers, etc.

Local Dance Halls

Masonic Hall, Garelochhead. Saturdays 1900–2300, 2s. 6d. (Special bus back).

British Legion Hall, Helensburgh. Fridays 2000–2300. Entrance by ticket only, 3s. 6d. (obtained at the Main Gate). No entrance after 2100.

18

Runs Ashore

Helensburgh Hotels: The Imperial; The Crown; The Station Bar; The Royal; The Clachan; The Rhuellen and The Kingsclere.

Garelochhead Hotels: The Garelochhead and The Anchor Bar.

Closing times: 2100 Winter; 2130 Summer.

Sunday opening of hotels holding a seven-day licence to 'Travellers' only, i.e., persons on the way from one place to another. (A book must be signed, stating where you are travelling to and from.)

Cinemas: TOWER, Colquhoun Square; LA SCALA, James St.

Church Services

On Board. The Chapel of St George.

Church Services are held on board on Sundays as follows:

Holy Communion: 0810.

Morning Prayer: 1015.

Evening Prayer – as announced.

Week-day Services – as announced.

Wives and Families are welcome to attend the Sunday Services. Those attending Church with their families may wear plain clothes.

The Squadron Chaplain is normally embarked in H.M.S. ADAMANT.

Ashore:

EPISCOPAL CHURCH – St Michael's; William St, Helensburgh. (In communion with Church of England.)
Holy Communion 0800, 1215 (first and third Sundays).
Morning Prayer 1100; Evening Prayer 1830.

CHURCH OF SCOTLAND – Shandon Parish Church (1½ miles) (Presbyterian).
Morning Service 1030; Evening Service 1830 (first and third Sundays).

Rev. Crichton Robertson – Officiating Minister, Church of Scotland and Free Churches, Gareloch Area (Rhu 213).

19

the day'. The 'jaunty's' eyes would be flashing and licking his lips at the prospect!

Jan survived the ordeal and two days later was asking the ward room steward if he could get the officers' birth dates as he had a plan to enroll them all in a children's club sponsored by one of the daily newspapers!

Madeira Shore Patrol

At the start of a six-month Falklands trip in the mid-1980s, the boat stopped little under a week out of Dolphin. It was a one-night stop, we had a chance to bathe just before we got in so that we were all nice and freshly washed (well sea washed anyway), before we got in. The captain decided to send out a shore patrol (a Navy thing – not really an O-boat thing) to keep us in check.

Everybody made it back OK, apart from the shore patrol, who were escorted back by the local police for being too loud and taking off their shirts.

Ronnie Ross, our disrespectful killick chef (who was always kept well out of the way of the end of patrol VIP) was always being picked up by the regulating staff in their capacity as fashion police. One day the Joss himself had reason to stop Ronnie, who addressed the joss as 'chief'. The apoplectic old fool exploded, and asked Ronnie to explain the significance of the metal badge on the sleeve of his woolly pully. He became even more enraged when Ronnie suggested that it denoted membership of the volunteer band.

Fore ends on an O-boat. Is he still waiting for the skipper's verdict?

three

'I say Number One, my end is diving… What the hell is your end doing?'

K-class engineering officer

While the majority of the Navy has had some difficulty in accepting the submariner as anything other than a nautical aberration, they had an equal amount of trouble accepting his method of underwater conveyance. In the early 1900s a very senior officer asked a submarine captain 'where he got the water from to dive his craft...' But in all fairness submariners have had some trouble in getting to grips with their crafts.

Admiral Fisher pointed out that 'The most fatal error imaginable would be to put steam engines in submarines', and nuclear submariners have spent a great deal of time and expended a substantial amount of energy in proving the truthfulness of that statement.

Periscopes were long, 7m (23ft) in an E-boat, and expensive at about £600 apiece (about £12,000 in today's money), although this was only a small fraction of what a modern instrument costs. A complete E-boat cost in the order of £306,000, the equivalent of £2.3m today, which is one fiftieth of the price of the latest British type 2400 diesel-electric boat commissioned in 1989.

The problem for periscope designers is twofold. Firstly, light had to be passed down through a very long thin tube without too much loss. Secondly, the tube had to be watertight and resistant to vibration. Not surprisingly, the technology of the time did not permit these aims to be met very well. Desication – drying out the tube by pressurised dry air – was difficult; the top window quickly got dirty (the British used duty-free gin to clean it), especially if there was any oil on the surface, and vision was frequently faulty.

Primitive periscopes (otherwise known as optical tubes, hyposcopes or cleptoscopes) were still installed in the older British boats when war came. Mistakes could arise when a captain was struggling to see a target: besides being constantly blurred, the horizon rotated when the instrument was trained around. On the beam it appeared vertical but astern it was horizontal and upside down. This was held by some to be a useful aberration because it indicated relative bearings; but on one well-known (per-war) occasion Lieutenant Ferdinand Feilman, commanding an A-boat in the Solent off Portsmouth, was trying to view an up-ended target when he glimpsed what he thought was the target's red flag. When he had turned and brought his tubes to bear he fired a torpedo. Unhappily, the flag turned out to be a very large pink parasol under which the wife of a retired colonel was sitting on Alverstoke beach. Ferdie made a perfect shot and the torpedo hit the shingle, running up alongside the terrified lady: the colonel sued the Admiralty for damages.

★ ★ ★

Just a quick one concerning a small slice of life aboard the King of the Fairies (HMS/M *Oberon* to you uneducated lot out there.)

After spending a few days down in jolly old Portland playing with our General Service friends and teaching them how to hunt, find and track submarines (let's hope the enemy always has at least one mast raised and showing eh?), we were despatched for our own index in Portland waters. Picture the nice relaxed scene: early morning, finished snorting, just drifting along about 90ft, no close sonar contacts, engines on the trim, engine room Tiffy is on the panel and the TI is on the planes. Engines, watching the bubble, says 'Looks like you're a bit light forward', so he tells the panel to trim forward slowly (as if you can). A short

Control room.

Eye-piece of a periscope in the conning tower of a submarine.

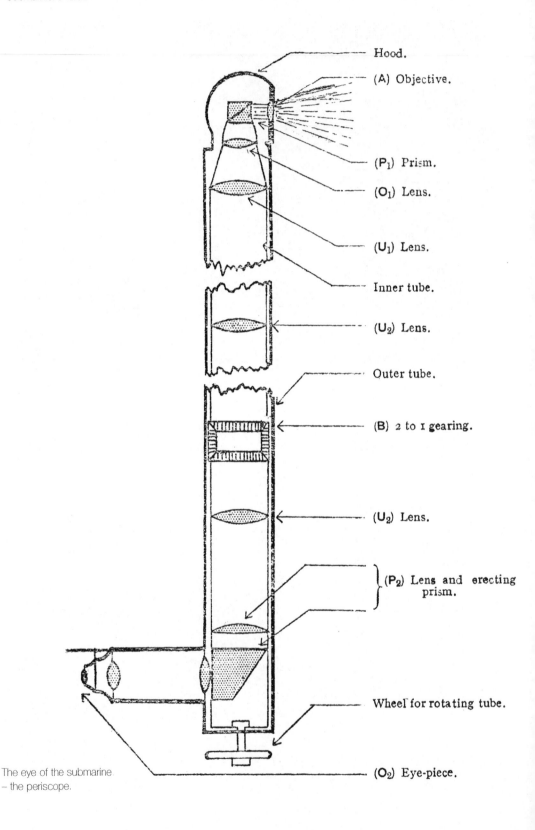

Hood.

(A) Objective.

(P₁) Prism.

(O₁) Lens.

(U₁) Lens.

Inner tube.

(U₂) Lens.

Outer tube.

(B) 2 to 1 gearing.

(U₃) Lens.

(P₂) Lens and erecting prism.

Wheel for rotating tube.

(O₂) Eye-piece.

The eye of the submarine
– the periscope.

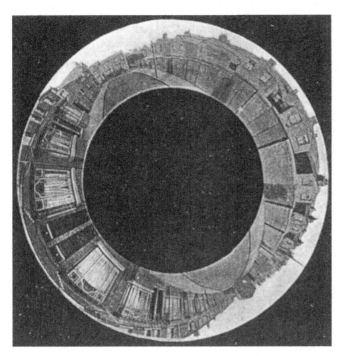

The continuous 'all-round-view' periscope.

time later after a bit of laughing and joking, in comes the torpedo officer and takes over the trim and just then the panel watch-keeper is also relieved so the watch goes on. Not too much later, the TI (who only passed his part three a couple of months ago) says 'Sir we are getting a bit heavy forward'. Torps, who liked to think he was a very experienced Sub/Lt in submarines, remarked that it seemed fine to him so there was obviously nothing wrong and get enough experience on the planes and you'll realise that. Another couple of attempts by the TI to gain some assistance got him nowhere. By this time he was trying to row on the planes to keep the bow up. At long last Torps realises that something is wrong as we are losing depth and the bow-down angle is getting quite severe. So in the time honoured tradition of trimming officers he speeds up. Nothing happens so he speeds up again, we are now full ahead group down when the panel watch-keeper realises we are still trimming forward and Captain comes out of his cabin

to find out what is happening. The captain was not quite quick enough to stop the torpedo officers' next move: if our speed is not enough to keep the bow up, let's stop the main motors to allow us to go group up. Bad move, the way comes off just in time for us to bottom and carve ourselves a nice little trench in the seabed. (I think it is now marked on Admiralty Charts as the 'Oberon Trench'.) It is surprising how quickly a crew can react to getting bulkheads, etc shut down while the bunrun is still trying to get off their thumbs. Moral of the story: give your relief a proper handover and at the very least, listen to the bloody planesman – after all, he is the one doing the rowing.

Just A Quaint Little *Osiris* Ditty

One time we were out at sea happily doing trials when it the time came to carry out our deep dive trial. We were at about 300ft, half ahead group down, when the captain gave the order 'Ten down keep 600ft'. So down we went as the angle came on and on and on. 'Planes jammed hard to dive!' cried the planes-man. 'Planes to hydraulic control, stop together, group up half ahead together, full rise on the planes!' No response, the boat was still heading down passing 600ft. 'Planes to amidships blow one and two main ballast tanks. Tanks blown angle coming off, boat coming up.' The captain then pipes 'Stand by to surface'

With the boat on the surface, everyone was happy. We had started to come back up at 670ft. It only came to light a few days later as no one had given it any real thought, but the day in question was Friday the 13th and what was HMS/M *Osiris's* pennant No?... S13.

★ ★ ★

There we were behaving ourselves at about 300ft or so, the best looking Porel in sub-marine command was doing maintenance in the radar shack when he heard the sound of gurgling water inside the pressure hull. Well, approximately two seconds later he was pass-ing the door to the ward room proving that a) the Porel is quicker than the eye, and b) adrenaline really is brown, lumpy and runny.

With the cries of 'fire the forward SSE (submerged signal ejector) and blow 1,2,4,6 and 7 main ballast tanks, blow 'Q', in fact, blow every bloody thing', we hit the roof about eleven seconds later. It was later discovered that while we were drifting along the captain had remarked that we would soon come up to periscope depth and start snorting. The elec-trical officer, who was on watch at the time, decided to check out the snort system and actually managed to drain down the snort mast at 300ft. This was the sound of gushing water we all heard and took to be flooding, I think Big L is still paying the laundry bill today.

★ ★ ★

The submarine, a Polaris boat, was on the surface in very rough weather. The LWEM (leading weapons electrical mechanic) came through the control room clutching a tot of gin. (Gin is the traditional periscope window cleaning agent). 'How are you going to get that up the fin in this weather?' asked the captain.

The LWEM downed the gin in one and dis-appeared up the ladder, the captains response was not recorded.

...and speaking of tots;

The submarine was up north on the surface, the weather was pretty rough. There was a casing rattle and it was decided that the ship's diver should go in and see if it could be fixed. The LMA (leading medical assistant) was the diver and when he was recovered, somewhat worse for wear, the chief doc gave the first lieutenant an update on his condition in the control room.

'He's not too bad sir, a couple of hours in his rack will see him OK'

'Bloody good effort' said the first lieutenant, placing a glass of rum on the chart table. The chief doc saw it off in one.

'That was for the bloody LMA!' roared the first lieutenant. The rest of the response was recorded but is unprintable.

★ ★ ★

Diesel submarines used to be very scared coming north from their sheltered bases in *Dolphin* or *Guzz*, as the dreaded Faslane tri-angle used to swallow them up.

Picture the scene HMS/M *Oberon* trying to sneak past sunny Faslane (ha ha) and head north for some jolly Mk8 firings in the Kyles. We had not sacrificed enough live babies or chickens to appease the great Faslane Gods, so mysterious faults started to

Control room – then. E-class submarine

Control room – now. V-class submarine

Engine room – then.

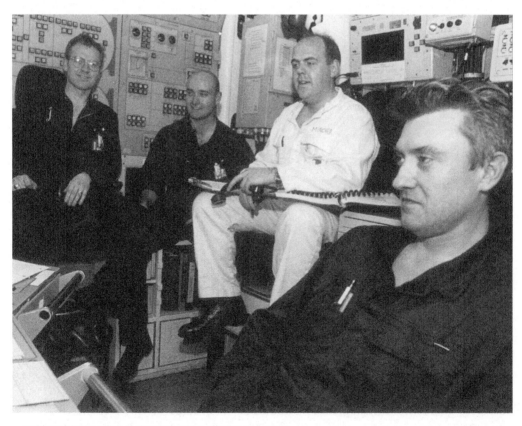

...and how it looks today. V-class submarine manoeuvring room.

appear. The fault that really got us was when the top bearing ring on the search periscope started to leak very badly, so the Faslane triangle got us yet again.

We went alongside and after much blood, sweat and tears repaired the bearing ring. Thinking ourselves lucky to get away so quickly, we sailed out, down past the Cumbraes and dived just off Arran. Ha! The bearing still leaked, we had not escaped Faslane just yet. To cut a long story short, we tried this idea of repairing the bearing ring, sailing down to Arran, diving, leaking and sailing back into Faslane four or five times until someone had the rather brilliant idea of allowing us to dive in the Gareloch as there is a rather deep trench running down the centre. There was a quiet air of peace and happiness aboard the *Oberon* that night as there was no early start for a dive to test the bearing as our dive in the Gareloch was planned for about eleven o'clock when there were no harbour move-

ments. So with such a relaxed atmosphere (for Faslane), most people ventured ashore to the sprawling metropolis of Helenburgh. Only the duty watch and the OA (ordnance artifer) remained on-board. Pity about the OA really, but he was just feeling his oats and was rather keen to try things on his own. He had just passed his part three exams three weeks beforehand, and the OA he relieved had used this time in Faslane to go on draft a few days early. So that fateful night the OA did some work all on his little lonesome. He blew up and drained down torpedo tubes one through to six and never actually told anyone, like the Jimmy, or even the engineer officer. The trot sentry would not have noticed the extra inch or so added to the draught marks during his rounds so nothing obvious was amiss. The submarine slept peacefully that night and awoke refreshed and ready for the new day. In the middle of the Gareloch, captains orders 'Stop together, group up, half ahead together, flood

Engine room in a *Holland* submarine.

Oil engines for driving the submarine up to the surface.

Q keep 90ft.' Orders carried out, the subma-rine was diving and the angle was coming on rather quickly. The depth gauge was also moving faster than expected, passing 150ft, the captain remarked to the Jimmy, 'Going down a bit fast aren't we No.1?' Jimmy replied 'like the proverbial stone sir, f★★★★★g sinking.' Well, after blowing everything going full astern, group up and full rise on everything as well, we regained the surface. Allowing for height differentials and all sorts of funny calculations for positioning our depth, we were about 9ft 6in from hitting the bottom of the Gareloch. I seem to remember the trench is about 350ft deep in the centre.

As for the O.A., well, after the full facts were discovered, it was thought kindest to return the poor misguided fellow back to the simpler life in General Service, to allow him to become a target again and leave the elite

in peace. Oh and to cap it all, the periscope bearing ring still leaked (it was finally repaired back in sunny *Dolphin*).

★ ★ ★

During the morning watch on HMS *Resolution* a routine quarterly main battery discharge was nearing completion. The Nuclear Chief of the Watch (NCOW), Tony McConnell was in the man room making preparations to connect the diesel generators as the battery voltage was approaching the minimum permissive voltage. Unfortunately on attempting to connect the first diesel generator, the breaker failed due to a defect. Not alarmed, the second diesel was flashed up. Unfortunately it sprung a significant fuel leak and had to be shut down immediately. With no method of charging the battery, it was now in fear of reversing polarity.

By this time, the fairly newly qualified Engineering Officer of the Day (EOOD), Nobby Clarke, had been made aware of the situation and having just woken up rushed into the man room in a state of severe panic (not uncommon). Clearly stressed by the problem, the NCOW invited the EOOD not to panic. 'Don't panic sir, sit down and assess the situation'. Happy to follow any advice on offer, he duly did this. After approximately two minutes the NCOW asked the EOOD if he had now assessed the situation. Having replied that he had, the NCOW said 'Excellent, now panic!!'

★ ★ ★

Sonar, the submarine's ears, has a long and eventful past. The passage of sound through water is a perverse science at best but over the years, the submariner has mastered this unruly technology.

The notable talent of Lieutenant Hamilton Harty RNVR (later Sir Hamilton, conductor of the Halle Orchestra) was enlisted to tune the equipment and match pairs of hydrophones. Anybody with a musical ear was an asset to underwater sound research, but one man deserves immortality, not so much for possessing perfect pitch, but for checking it with a precisely tuned cranium. Sir Richard Paget was convinced by 1916 that the key to hydrophone design was to establish propeller frequencies. Accordingly, he arranged to be suspended by his legs over the side of a boat in the Solent while a submarine circled him. After a suitable period submerged (and before he actually drowned) this devoted scientist was hauled up humming the notes he had heard whereupon, safely back in the boat, he related them to the standard G-sharp which he obtained by tapping his skull with a metal rod.

Electric motors used to propel the submarine when it is submerged.

Engine room. V-class submarine.

Sound room. V-class submarine.

Cleaning Windows

★ ★ ★

As it spun on a SOCA weekend in the Atlantic bar (JR's mess) Dolphin *by an old submariner.*

During the Second World War, I was asked by the captain to volunteer to go up the find and clean the periscope windows/lens. He said it was a risky business, and if a German boat or ship turned up, he would have to dive. 'Ok' I said, we surfaced and up I went with the casing tower hatch shut behind me. The job was done and down came the captain. He patted me on the back and said 'Well done, that was a risky job'. 'Not really' I said, "cause I've got the main vent panel fuses in my back pocket!'

Back afties are great practical jokers who cannot help but smile when we think back to such merry pranks such as sending 'electric bills' to the ship's company, or the side-splitting times having part threes running around trying to get wood for the for'd burner. But occasionally it goes wrong and when it does...

The chief tiff on a Polaris boat sent a young part-three MEM to the ship's medics to see if he could get a fallopian tube. The medics told him they didn't have any but they thought there were some in 3 berth store. The young MEM duly arrived there and was asked if he required a left or right fallopian tube. 'Don't know', answered the MEM, 'Well best you find out laddie' said the ever-helpful LSA. The young MEM reported back to the chief tiff, 'A left one lad, everybody uses left ones'. 'Haven't got any left ones', said the LSA, 'you'll have to go up to the main stores'. Off set the MEM. 'Sterile or non sterile?' asked the pre-warned main storekeeper. 'Don't know', answered the MEM. 'Well best you find out laddie', said the positively gloating storeman. 'Sterile for god's sake', said the chief tiff, 'don't they teach you nowt these days?' 'Sterile eh?' said the storeman, 'now that's a shame, a lad off an S-boat took the last one just a few minutes ago. I've got a 5/8s non-sterile left-handed one if that will do?' '5/8s eh', said the chief tiff, 'see if they can do it in non-sterile butt ended'...

'Butt ended' said the storeman... Some time later the chief tiff took pity on the young stoker, 'Tell me lad,' he said in his best fatherly voice, 'do you know what a fallopian is?' 'It's part of the female reproductive system

chief'. 'Well, why for christ's sake have you been walking about all morning trying to find one?!!' 'Well, chief, while I've been walking about in the sun everybody down here has been scrubbing out for captain's rounds!' ...from the mouths of babes.

★ ★ ★

SCENE: Control Room Nuclear Submarine at Sea.

Problem with the Attack Scope, stuck in the well, a tiff had been working on it for some time without result...

The chief stoker comes on watch unaware of the problem...

OOW: 'What do you think is wrong with the mast, chief?'

Chief stoker: 'Well sir, having just looked at the problem, I think the screwdown, no return, reciprocating, heliomagnetic, oscillating, transforming, conductors, isolating, relief valves, spindle sprocket has got a bit of sh one

Commanding officer's station, showing controls, in a *Holland* submarine.

t on it, or in other words... How the F★★K should I know? I've just come on watch.'

★ ★ ★

SCENE: HMS Dreadnought *at sea, mid-atlantic; ship's company have been told the S/M will remain on patrol and not go to Florida for a jolly.*

Main Broadcast: 'Safeguard safeguard... man overboard'.

After some 30 minutes the man is picked up, an LMEM (leading marine engineering mechanic).

OOD (in the fin): 'Why did it take so long to find him chief?'

Chief: 'Well sir I'm not saying the JRs are unhappy but when we picked him up he was swimming AWAY from the boat.'

★ ★ ★

I was working in the torpedo guidance control workshop. Tony Knowles was the chief OA in charge. I was hoping the *aneus* would come in so I could complete my part three. Anyway *Olympus* had come in. She was the first O-boat with this TCS – electronic –. Anyway they had a problem with one of the tubes, the link from the tube door to the disconnect switch, at the far end of the tube (big long cable) with sixty-five pin connections in it. There were, supposedly, some breaks in the cable but they didn't know where – they didn't have any drawings. So I, as the new PO, waiting to get a part three, and this killick REM got sent down to sort this out. So there were no drawings. The plug was no problem because it was just a straightforward plug but we didn't know where all the sixty-five pins went into the disconnect switch. So the idea was for me to get up and disconnect it, take one cable at a time, earth it out, and make a couple of leads on to the mega. So

all I had to do was slide on the pin, clip it onto the door to make an earth, swing through. Therefore the minute we got the connection, we could say that that pin went to number whatever in the disconnect switch. So I got up. I was on the second tube, forward port, up top. So I got up there to get to the disconnect switch – not a complicated situation. Anyway once you get yourself wedged in there, you're going to stay there. I disconnected the first one, earthed it out, and of course, you have to go through every piece – sixty-five pins – until you are through. Anyway, I finally got through in the end.

'No, nothing'.

'Are you sure?'

'Yeah.'

'Okay then we'll try another. I'll put this one back. I'll disconnect another one and swing through again.'

So off we went again. Still nothing. I was shouting down at him and I said,

'I wonder if we have been unlucky with the first two of the two broken ones.'

'No it can't be – I have never been that lucky in my life. We will just try one more'.

Anyway I earthed it out, he was going away!! He still got nothing. Then Tony Knowles, the chief O.A., came in the forend. He had just come through the door by the hatch in the door!!

'What the f★★★ is going on?'

So I replied, 'We tried' (shouting from the corner of the second tube) 'we are trying to figure out where these leads go so that I can make a diagram, but we're not having much luck at the moment, the first three we've chosen aren't giving a reading.'

He said 'Yeah, well why don't the pair of you get on the same f★★★★★★ tube then.'

I was on the second tube and he was on the fourth tube.

★ ★ ★

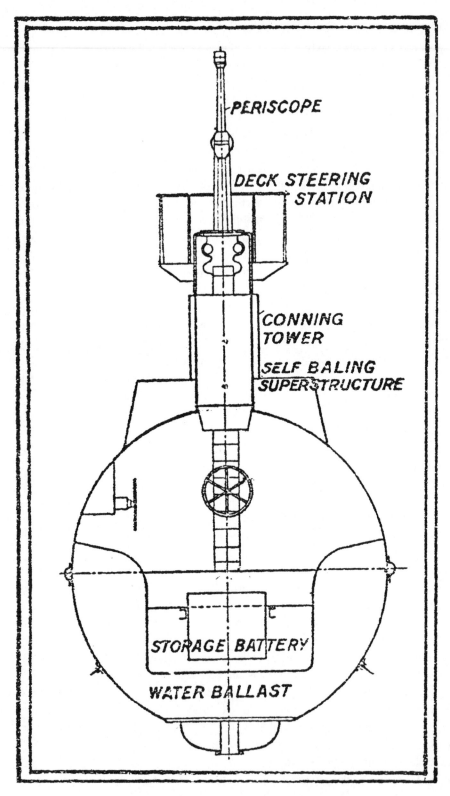

PERISCOPE

DECK STEERING
STATION

CONNING
TOWER

SELF BALING
SUPERSTRUCTURE

STORAGE BATTERY

WATER BALLAST

Sectional view
through the
conning tower
of a *Holland*
submarine,
showing the
circular form of
hull.

Trimming has been a constant and seemingly unsolvable problem to the submariner, it has led to such control room scenes as:

Ship control officer of the watch: How's the trim, afterplanesman?

Afterplanesman: 'How's the *Titanic*?

Afterplanesman to forplanesman: Who put this trim on – Rubic?

★ ★ ★

In late 1971 I was a sub-lt undergoing part three training in HMS *Porpoise*. On one, never to be forgotten day, the CO allowed me to dive the submarine from the bridge for the first time. Crisply passing the appropriate order to 'dive the submarine' via the voice pipe to the control room, I took a final 'all round look' at the surface ships in the vicinity, cleared the bridge with my look-out and descended through the tower to the control room below, taking care to shut, clip, pin and report the 'Upper Lid' on the way down. On arrival below, I noted with great satisfaction that everything was happening in copybook fashion with all personnel closed up and, from the bow-down angle, the submarine was clearly descending, as intended, to the depths below. I was just making my formal report to the CO with some pride when there was an enraged howl from the coxswain at the helmsman's position as his left ear took a full bore of seawater from the voice pipe. My pride turned to immediate humiliation with the realization that, in my haste, I had committed that cardinal sin of failing to shut the upper voice pipe cock on vacating the bridge. Whilst the CO calmly said to me 'well, you won't make that mistake again', the coxswain was less generous. He loathed me with a vengeance thereafter and would only speak to me through intermediaries, referring to me as 'the effing part three subby'. So much for the old adage of 'all buddies in boats'!

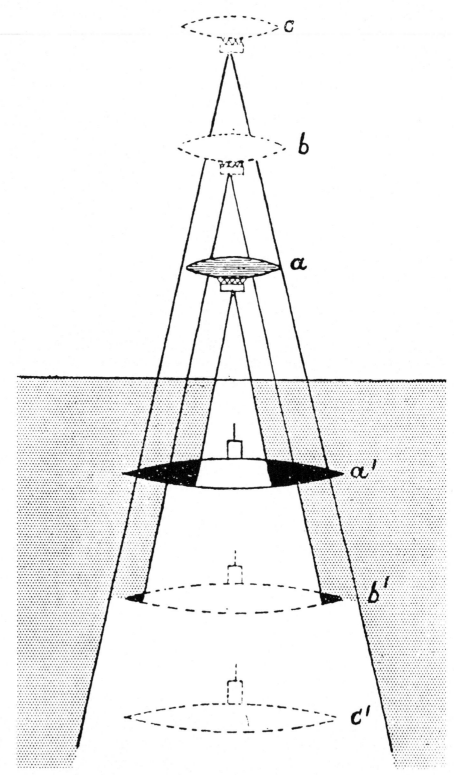

Spotting a submarine from above. Even in 1915 the 'Fleet Air Arm' still required lessons on finding submarines.

Attack teams

four

No occupation for a gentleman

Tales From Barrow-In-Furness

Windy and Brighams' sacred tipster.

The earlier submarines had such small crews that there was, of necessity, a great deal of cross training, a trait that is still evident in part three training. Without a dedicated signal-man, the Admiralty felt it necessary in 1905 to issue a Fleet Instruction advising the surface fleet to 'send to submarines slowly'.

One In Two

In the '70s, bombers had the 'luxury' of a one in three watch-keeping system. As a young sailor at the time I remember the intricacies of West Country – one in three meaning going to bed at strange times when I wasn't tired and being dragged out of bed when I was, all very confusing – but the pace of life on a bomber is best described as slow and the system was workable.

When we sailed for work-up however, things had to change. Our First Lieutenant Robin Gee, was going to take a leaf out of the SSN (ship submersible nuclear) book and we were going to have a two-watch system. Great, six on and six off, simple. The change was announced on daily orders, which stated that at one o'clock in the afternoon the submarine would go into the two-watch system.

At twelve o'clock in the afternoon, the TASO, a remarkable Irishman, called Paddy (Nail Bomb) Johnson, made the following pipe on main broadcast in a very broad Irish accent:

'D'ya hear dere, der submarine will go into two watches in one hour's time, first watch will be on first. If yer not in first watch, find out which watch yer in!'

Hysteria followed.

Most submariners remember Barrow-in-Furness with great fondness. It is a small, self-contained, industrial northern town with more pubs per square inch than anywhere else in the British Isles. Add the cheapest beer prices and friendly underpaid people to this equation and the fact that pusser gave every man a fortune to find accommodation, then it's easy to understand why matelots had the life of kings here.

The Britannia public house, was the sailors' social base at this time. The owner, Bill Healey, was a mountain of a man, ex-paratrooper from the war, ex-rugby league player, capped many times for England and all round bigot in the true fashion of Alf Garnett, but very lovable just the same. Bill, along with his wife Marie, took in sailors. The accommodation was good and Bill ensured that good old-fashioned army standards were maintained by his residents. Marie on the other hand was everyone's mother from home, a gem of a lady in every sense of the word and loved by all that made her acquaintance.

Bill had a weakness, not unreasonable for a publican; it was the sport of kings, horse-racing. Regular daily reading for Bill was *Sporting Life* and any paper containing form. So ensnared by his passion, Bill even subscribed to a 'professional' tipster who he rang daily in Liverpool. Now Bill was also a businessman, and anyone that threatened his livelihood was not going to get his good side. The Salvation Army stopped trying to raise donations in the Brit after Bill took issue on their stance on temperance, and unceremoniously ejected two old ladies from the public bar, hurling their copies of *War Cry* and collecting tins after them.

Windy and Brigham were two POs in the honest branch, Windy an SA and Brigham a

V-class submarine.

chef. They were frequent visitors to the Brit, more frequent than they were to the yard in fact and good pals with Bill. Like Bill they also enjoyed the sport of kings, but when it came to winning, Bill always had the edge. Being proper sporting gentlemen, they were never boastful about their winnings, of course. Except Bill, who took every opportunity to show that in the macho world of horse-racing, he was without doubt the very best there was! Indeed a local authority even.

One day Windy and Brigham decided to have some fun with Bill. They made a note of all the outside, long odds winners in the previous week's racing. With the help of a typewriter and a copy of the *War Cry* the game was on. The *War Cry* was not a well-printed magazine and it was easy to type into a small space 'Joahna's Tip for the week!' Surprise, surprise it was always a fifty to one winner.

With a copy of the doctored magazine in hand, the pair went to the Brit at lunchtime and decided to read carefully the word of the Salvation Army. Their focus on it was so pronounced that eventually it got Bill's attention. 'What's that you have there lads?' When told, Bill was less than pleased and issued the sort of remarks aimed to question the intellect and legitimacy of the two lads. True to form, the lads tried to argue that you should have an open mind, not to prejudge and that maybe there was something in it. Bill stormed off! A little while later and some way through the magazine, Brigham calls to Bill and asks,

An officer
mustering
the ventilation
staffs on his
submarine.

'What won at Kempton last Wednesday in the three-fifteen?' Bill's interest was restored,

'Well do you know?' says Bill, 'It was an unheard of outsider, came in at fifty to one. I think it was Davy's Mate or something, big shock to everyone that!'

'I don't believe it,' says Brigham, 'That's just what Joahna's Tip for the week is'.

A very shocked Bill doesn't believe it and asks to see the *War Cry*. Sure enough, there in front of his eyes is 'Joahna's Tip for the week'. Still not fully convinced Bill goes about his work with just a little flea in his ear.

The following week saw the same pattern of events, Windy and Brigham together with a week old, doctored *War Cry* sat musing over its contents in the public bar of the Brit. It didn't take too long to get Bill's attention this time and he was less abusive, but hovered at their end of the bar. Eventually impatience got the better of the poor old landlord and he asked the question, 'What's Joahna's Tip for the week then?' Windy and Brigham searched the pages; low and behold they found it – another outsider with very long odds. Again, Bill scrutinized the *War Cry*, he looked completely gobsmacked and the cogs of his brain began to turn. 'Joahna's Tip for the week' was gaining a lot of interest and it was time for Windy and Brigham to tell the rest of the sailors in the building group, just what was going on.

Bill Healey was also doing some thinking; he was desperate to get the latest edition of the *War Cry*. Before an evening of pub-crawling or nightclubbing all the sailors would muster at the Brit as a starting point. Bill usually enticed the lads to stay, but recently he had been wishing them on their way and as a parting shot one evening, gave one of the lads a pound and asked that if they came across the Sally Army, to get a copy of the *War Cry* for him. This was odd for someone known for his arch right style of generosity. However, he did get a copy of the fated magazine, but cunningly it was a week out of date and included 'Joahna's Tip for the week'. Keeping up with the scam took a concerted effort and was fraught with danger, but the effect it was having on the lovable old bruiser, of a landlord was simply amazing.

Bill called the local Sally Army, and even offered a sizeable donation if only they would add his pub to the list of places to visit during the week. They never came. One Saturday, always a big race day, Brigham and Windy were sat at the bar of the Brit. A man walked in and in exchange for a £5-note handed over a copy of the *War Cry* to Bill. Our two boys were nothing if not courageous. They sat it out. Bill took large volumes of ridicule for his reading material and was visibly more interested in its contents than his customers. After almost an hour of searching, he still couldn't find 'Joahna's Tip for the week'. He handed to our two lads and asked for their help. They must have missed it out this week they suggested. Bill was not a happy bear; he had just paid a fiver for this valuable piece of racing form, and to Bill, racing is a serious business. After another hour Bill, having festered enough, picked up the *War Cry*, gave it a quick scan, found what he was looking for and reached for the phone in the bar. 'Hello, is that the Citadel in London, yeah well where is Joahna's Tip for the week then, you seem to have left it out this week?' A long silence followed, Bill's head went down, the back of his neck turned red, reminding the lads of his links with the Paras, and they exited the Brit before Bill replaced the receiver.

Bill did eventually forgive Windy and Brigham and removed the bar on them after about three months but they had to endure years of abuse for their little scam. Bill learned only one thing: Never trust a MATELOT!!!!

★ ★ ★

Early in 1948 I was serving as 'Tanky' on the submarine *Amphion* which was ordered home from Hong Kong. Singapore was our first stop on the way home in company with the depot ship *Adamant* and another submarine *Astute*. The trip to Singapore only took a week so the stores on-board were only for that period, which left lots of room in the freezers, etc. The fridge and freezer on an A-class submarine are down below the main deck in the auxiliary machinery space, entry being on the starboard side outside the ward room and the fridge and freezers over on the port side. On the Saturday evening just before our arrival in 'Singas', on a perfectly calm night I went below to get the pork out for the next day's dinner. Seeing two nice legs of port at the back of the freezer I stepped inside to get them. At this precise moment the boat gave a little roll and lo and behold it was enough to slam the freezer door shut. What I should say here is that the doors were self-locking and there I was in complete darkness inside. After pounding on the door with a leg of pork I soon realised that nobody would hear me over the noise made by the auxiliary machinery! I should also mention that being in the tropics, I was only wearing a pair of shorts. In despair and without much hope I gave one more pounding on the door, when the door was suddenly flung open! I was never so glad to see the ward room steward in all my life. He had quite by accident come down to the fridge to get cheese out for the ward room dinner. The look of surprise on his face on seeing me was classic!! I had been in the freezer for about half an hour and had it not been for the steward, nobody would have missed me until the following morning when the chef looked for the meat for the day. A tot off the cox'n and a good night's sleep soon put me right but it was a close shave.

★ ★ ★

On the *Seascout* in 1951 (Tanky again!) we were running from Invergordon doing A/S work with the RAF and as usual it was as rough as hell whilst waiting for the RAF to make up its mind whether the weather was good enough for them to fly or not. One fore-noon watch we lost the steward, we couldn't find him anywhere, it was his first boat out of training and weighed about eight stone. At one stage we thought he had gone up on the bridge and gone over the side somehow. He was as sick as a dog every time there was a slight ripple. To cut a long story short, we found him in the fore ends squeezed down between the ship's side and a Mk8 torpedo. How he got there nobody knows but we had to roll out the torpedo to get him out! The 'Jimmy' (Lieut. M. Todd) said 'pour a cup of soup into him, that'll keep him alive till we get back to harbour'.

★ ★ ★

'What's this chef?'
'How should I know, I'm a cook not a detective!!'

★ ★ ★

'Why do they call wreckers – wreckers?'
'Cos the first one wasn't very good'

★ ★ ★

During DED on a nuclear S/M, a party of submariners were 'man handling' the Fwd APD to the main access for translex from the S/M. As the team was preparing the APD for lifting out, they were interrupted...

Down the ladder came...

1. A silver handbag, followed by...
2. A pair of silver shoes, followed by...

On the conning tower.

3. A Lady dressed in a silver evening gown, followed by…
4. A senior medical officer in mess undress.

They clambered over the APD, lifting ropes, blocks and tackles and pumps and pipes and assembled rating and proceeded to the ward room.

The duty engineer looked startled and said 'Can I help you Sir?'
'Yes', said the senior medical officer.
'What time is the ward room party ?'
'It's next Thursday sir' said the duty officer.

★ ★ ★

SCENE: HMS Dolphin *defaulters, CDRs table.*
In the dark days of station cards.
A chief has been 'weighed off' by the CDR and given three days stoppage of leave and pay.

Crime – three minutes adrift (three minutes).

CDR: 'Have you anything to say chief?'
At this point the chief bends down and looks under the table.
CDR: 'What the devil are you looking for chief?'
Chief: 'Justice sir', there's non-coming over the top. (He got seven days 9s as well).

★ ★ ★

SCENE: 'S'-*class S/M alongside in gib.*

First day the ship's company JRs had been taking a lot of 'flak' (from General Service ratings from three or four Ships Trotted Fund) about S/M pay, subsistance etc, etc, paid to submariners.
Second day the JRs were now well and trully 'brassed off'.

23:59: A road sign from outside HMS *Rook* which read:

CAUTION, ROAD
LIABLE TO SUBSIDANCE

was pinched and taken on-board the S/M.

Third day next day on the fwd casing, a large sign said:

CAUTION, SUBMARINERS
LIABLE TO SUBSIDANCE

The sign was allowed to stay on the fwd casing much to the merriment of the ship's company and much to the chagrin of the skimmers.

One Hand From Aft

On one O-boat, we amused ourselves making sealion crests. As the weeks went by the plaster stuff was shoved into different moulds for amusement, one being a yellow plastic glove.

When we surfaced after a month dived, the usual pipe went out:

'One hand to man the blower – from aft'.

So duly, the plaster hand made its way into the control room from the aft mess and landed at the training officer's feet – he was not amused.

★ ★ ★

The steward came into the sick bay one afternoon, and, peering through the cloud of smoke (with which myself and Josh Tetley were trying to bring about the early demise of the doctor) managed to make out the outline of the doctor in the fog, and asked him if he wanted sweet or savoury following his main course at dinner that evening. The doctor replied 'steward – you know very well that I'm a duff officer'.

★ ★ ★

Scribes was once told (or so he claimed) by an XO to type up a very secret document, with the specific instruction not to read it whilst doing so…

five

Practically perfect in every way

Mary Poppins

The 'sea daddy' nature of the counselling that a young submariner receives in his formative years ensures no matter where his head finishes up, his feet are always firmly on the ground. This guidance continues throughout his career, often paying little heed to rank or seniority.

It's a game anybody can play.

A few years ago my son and I were hoping to find a sunken steam boat in the Clyde called the *Osprey*. It had been 'run down' by a paddle steamer off Kilcreggan pier about 100 years ago.

When the Clyde was re-surveyed, a 'wreck' mark appeared in the channel approximately where the *Osprey* was rammed. I decided to ring the cartographer at Taunton to see if they could give me any further information. A lady answered the phone, I must have had on my 'Oh God it's a woman' voice. I patiently explained I was a submariner and wanted information about a wreck in the Clyde and this was probably man's business. She asked me which chart the wreck was on.

'The one with Greenock on', I answered.

'What?' She replied.

'Here we go', I thought.

'It's the one with Greenock near the bottom and Dumbarton up on the left', I patiently explained.

'Have you got the chart in front of you?' she asked.

'Yes'.

'In the bottom right hand corner there is a number in black bold letters. Could you tell me what it is then I can go and get the chart'.

Once that was sorted out she said 'could you give me the position of the wreck?'

'Course I can', I confidently replied, we were now firmly in man's territory.

'Can you see Greenock?

'Well, if you go up about 2in and across 1½ in...'

'What?' the lady said.

'Here we go again', I thought. I patiently explained where the wreck was.

'Oh you mean 51.47 N, 27.67 W', she cockily interrupted.

'Oh yer, that's it', slyly hiding the fact I hadn't a clue what she was talking about.

The lady was really helpful and informative and when she'd finished I thanked her profusely.

'No trouble at all' she said, 'but do you mind if I ask you a question?'

'Of course not, you've been more than helpful, it's the least I could do', I snivelled.

'At the start you said you were a submariner?'

'Yes'.

'They don't let you drive it do they?' she asked.

'No'.

'Thank God for that!'

★ ★ ★

At sea I kept the night watches, every third night my morning watch would coincide with my good buddy John Pounder, and as is the custom, we'd scrub out the tunnel and manoeuvring flat. While we whiled away the twilight hours we'd put the world to rights, and anything else for that matter. During a Christmas and New Year patrol several years ago I received an award in the New Year's Honours List. Not too far into the New Year, I was scrubbing the tunnel with John when I said,

'There'll have to be some changes, now I've got the BEM'.

'Quite right' said John, 'you wash and I'll dry!'

★ ★ ★

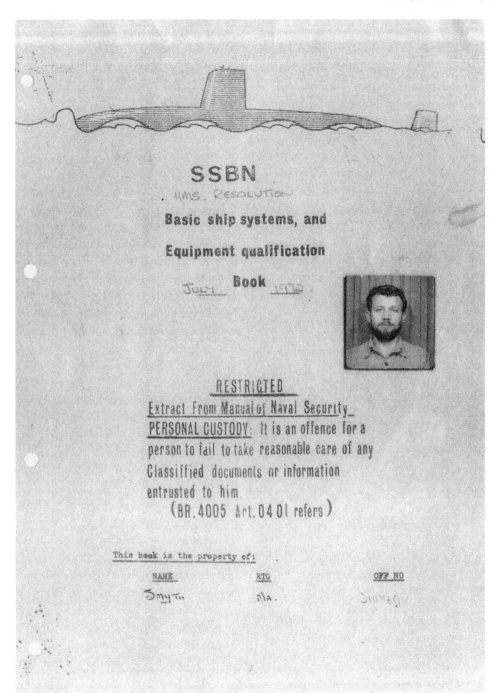

SSBN

. HMS. RESOLUTION

Basic ship systems, and

Equipment qualification

JULY Book 1972

RESTRICTED

Extract From Manual of Naval Security
PERSONAL CUSTODY: It is an offence for a
person to fail to take reasonable care of any
Classified documents or information
entrusted to him.
(BR.4005 Art.04 01 refers)

This book is the property of:

NAME	RTG	OFF NO
Smyth	MA.	D111769

A part three book – in the early days of submarines, members of a small crew had to understand and be able to operate all the equipment on-board. This rationale has been applied throughout the service's history.

I had just completed the 100ft free accent in the tank and was waiting for a bus. With hindsight that only years can bring, I must have looked, at best, a prat. Resplendent in brand new submarine blazer; submarine tie; submarine socks; 'I'm a submariner' scrawled on my pusser's grip. In retrospect 'prat' is putting a gloss on my appearance I certainly didn't deserve. There was an old man waiting at the bus stop, he looked me up and down, quite understandably and said,

'You in the Navy son?'

'Navy?' I replied, 'Navy! I'm a submariner!'

'Oh' said the old man, 'I was in submarines'.

'What's that' I asked 'S- and T-boats in the last war?'

'No' he replied. 'K-boats'.

One young brand new submariner put firmly in his place.

★ ★ ★

Overheard in the control room:

'I'm sorry chief, I can't quite place the accent.'

'No.4 Pier Road, sir.'

★ ★ ★

'Honest doc, I've broke me arm.'

'Well it must be a simple fracture.'

'Why's that?'

'It seems to think it's a bruise!'

★ ★ ★

SCENE: *Division Officer Interview.*

(For info: Cattedown is an area of Plymouth famous for its scrap yards, foreign eating parlours and Edwardian houses.)

Officer: I see by your 264's chief, you were in the Falklands conflict.

Chief: Yes sir, I was at Tumbledown when the first shot was fired... And I was at Cattedown when the second one was.

Officer: Very funny chief, how many A-levels have you?

Chief: Fourteen sir …

Officer Don't be silly, chief …

Chief: You started it, sir ….

★ ★ ★

Many years ago in 1944 a young lad joined the Royal Navy. At seventeen and a half, he realised his ambition and trotted of to HMS *Royal Arthur* (Skegness) to join and be kitted up, etc, eventually ending up at HMS *Ganges* (Shotley), for his basic training. Part of his induction was to have a lecture on the uses of the sick bay in the RN and remembers well the old chief saying 'if you are sick, go sick, that is what the sick bay is for!' Part of this lecture also, was to receive his first ever vaccination against smallpox.

The first part of his training was square bashing and one afternoon he became light headed with a terrible headache, but stuck it out until the next morning after enduring a terrible night of sweating and all his bones aching. He had never felt like this before and just couldn't understand it!

Deciding he was sick he reported to the sick bay. A two-badge leading sick bay tiffy and a petty officer spent half an hour trying to convince him that he was only malingering and trying to get out of square bashing. Insisting that he was sick he eventually saw a surgeon lieutenant commander RNVR who prescribed two aspirins and back to duty. Needless to say, that same day at half past eleven he collapsed in a big heap on the parade ground. He then spent a week in *Ganges'* sick quarters where he was diagnosed as suffering from vaccine fever pumped full of the new fangled antidote, penicillin. (10,000 units I believe), that's probably why I never went CDA in my next forty-one years of service!

Polaris missile compartment.

That sailor was of course, me and as you can imagine, I was not very impressed with RN sick bays! Forty-one years later when I retired from the RN and the RAN and after seeing and attending innumerable naval doctors and 'pusser's' sick bays in that time, I have never seen anything to change that impression!

★ ★ ★

After I left Mountbatten's staff in 1954 I was drafted as scratcher of HMS/M *Sanguine* and on a visit to Yugoslavia we went to Dubrovnik (still ruled by Tito) where the Yugoslav Army arranged for half the crew, in turn, to go camping. Outside the town they had set up a special area with two-man tents, barbeque area and latrines, etc. They also provided a trailer loaded with wood for the fires and

a trailer tank full of fresh water. The next morning they came round and asked what we required for the next twenty-four hours and we replied another trailer full of wood. They gave us a funny look but did as we asked. This went on for the four days we were there, asking for more wood each day until, when we where leaving, they explained that they thought the wood would last us the four days and they would have to replenish the trailer of water each day, hence the funny looks! They obviously didn't know much about submariners!!

★ ★ ★

When Admiral of the Fleet Earl Moutbatten of Burma retired as the chief of defence staff, he travelled around most of the UK to give

Everybody wants to be a submariner.

a farewell speech, and to meet 'old ships' men he had served with during his career. Lots of people knew that I had spent nearly two years with him so I was detailed off to attend HMS *Sultan* with a party from HMS *Dolphin*, and become an 'old ship' so to speak. Knowing what he was like I was not too keen on this but didn't have much say in it!

After his speech, about fifteen of us lined up to be introduced to the earl. I was at the far end of the line. He started as usual, shook hands and said 'Who are you, where did we serve together? Ah yes, I remember' etc. Until he arrived at me. 'Lilliman', he said, 'never thought you would make a coxswain', and promptly walked off without even a handshake!

By the same token, when I was serving in the RAN as officer in charge of the fire department on Garden Island dockyard, Sydney, Mountbatten was scheduled to catch a helicopter from Garden Island to visit HMAS *Nirimba* on the outskirts of Sydney. Being an aircraft operation, we had to provide a fire party. Soon after the arrival of the 'chopper', Mountbatten arrived accompanied by Rear Admiral Dovers RAN, Flag Officer East Australian Area. I opened the car door and giving one of my better naval salutes said

'Remember me sir, your diver in Malta?'

'Lilliman' he said, 'you're looking prosperous' he said, putting his arms around me, virtually giving me a hug. He then started talking about our fishing experiences while the admiral was practically dragging him to the 'chopper' with me trailing along!

Two hours later, on his arrival back at Garden Island, after getting out of the 'chopper' he shook the pilot's hand. Then he made a beeline for me and started talking about Malta, once more with the admiral dragging him to the car explaining they were half an hour behind schedule and Mountbatten had to catch a plane back to the UK. At least I can say he never forgot me!

★ ★ ★

Asking the chief stoker to partner me in the mess crib competition he replied,

'I can't play crib'

'Twenty years in the Navy and you can't play crib?'

'I've been busy' he replied.

★ ★ ★

At action stations, 'Missile', the leading cook had nothing to do, so on hearing the pipe he rushed into the control room and said to the captain, 'Galley oven shut and clipped sir'. The skipper said 'leading cook at every change of the watch and at every exercise, you will report to the control room with that report, until further notice'.

After about four days his flippant remark was not so funny.

★ ★ ★

Heard in the control room:

'Why have we surfaced?'

Young MEM: I think we surfaced to blow round ★★★★★★.

K-boats in Algeria.

six

It's the same the whole world over...

Submarine Service Centennial Celebrations

As you read this, the above celebrations in HM Naval Base Clyde are well and truly behind us but I thought you might like to know the sorts of things that happened during the week, 28 May through to 4 June 2001.

Three members of the west of Scotland branch of the Submariners Association spent the entire week in the base, Bob Cantley, Gracie Gerc and myself, Jim McMaster. We decided that as the boats were due to start arriving early on the Monday morning (28 May) we should go to the base on the Sunday. Just so that we could be settled in before the boats arrived, you understand!!

First to arrive on Monday morning was the French boat FS *Saphir* and of course the jetty area was a busy place with berthing party, welcoming officers, interpreters, sightseers and us!

Bob Cantley was probably the first one to get a 'Grippo' from the French. I think it was the splendid sight of Bob in all his finery that caught the eye of the French sailor. Trust Bob to find the only Frenchman who cannot speak English!! The remainder will remain our secret, Bob, although Gracie and I did wonder where you got the baguette and long sausage.

It wasn't long before the spotlight fell upon the approaching RFV *Vologda* as it glided up the loch. The sight of a Russian Kilo-class submarine sailing into Faslane is not something you see regularly!! By this time the jetty was busier than Argyle Street on a Saturday afternoon as everyone gathered in the vicinity of the Russian's berth. As the *Vologda* sailed into Neptune there were three cine cameras in full action on her bridge so the Russians missed no one and nothing. From the moment the gangway was across, there was an almost continuous stream of officers either going aboard or coming ashore. Unfortunately most of the other boats arriving received little or no attention as all eyes were focussed on the *Vologda*.

I'm sure I wasn't the only one surprised to find that the hats worn by Russian officers and senior rates really are as huge as they appear on TV etc. These are seriously big hats!!

Other boats started to arrive at regular intervals and the whole thing calmed down after a while until the Spanish boat SPS *Tramontana* pulled alongside. The surprise there was that one of their casing party was a female (Bob thought it was just a pretty boy...) and this of course attracted a lot of attention. That was a pity for the Spaniard who slipped off the casing into the loch. He would rather have had no one see that. Luckily it was to the outboard side so he was OK. (They have two females in their crew)

The USS *Tennessee* duly arrived and blanked out the sun as she slid along the loch heading for the very secure section of the base. This boat is 31m longer than our Trident boats – A big submarine. Our American cousins were generally anonymous during the week with only one or two being spotted around the place.

Eventually there were twelve foreign boats alongside and very impressive it looked. The Canadians didn't make it as they broke down and had to put into Campbeltown, and for all we know she could still be there! Canada was bringing HMCS *Unicorn,* one of the upholder class bought from us, to the party. Did they never wonder why we sold them these boats for $1 each??

So the first day was taken up with the arrival of all these boats.

Tuesday was the start of the many visits and tours arranged for the visitors. Most of

Divisions preparing to 'match' on at the Centennial Celebrations at Faslane.

Smart as a submariner?

Up periscope!

the crews were living in hotels dotted all over the place so the vast majority of people on the organised tours were Russian and Polish. Available tours on Tuesday were to the Wallace Monument, Stirling Castle, Ibrox and Parkhead.

Bob, Gracie and I went with the group visiting Ibrox and Parkhead. The first obstacle was getting out of the North Gate. When all the group were finally assembled at the Quarry car park we made our way by coach to the gate only to find that several of the Russians did not have their passports with them so the nice policeman sent us all back to get the documents!! After all these years trying to get into the nuclear submarine base, these Russian submariners were having trouble getting out!

We arrived at Ibrox more than two hours late so our tour guide had gone, however the commissionaire at the front door suggested that we go up to the restaurant for lunch while he searched for another guide. The Russians and the Poles were very, very impressed with the Argyle Restaurant, which on match days, forms the hospitality suites and overlooks the pitch. Everyone enjoyed a splendid carvery and the staff made a right fuss of the guests. The crews appeared to be very young particularly the Russian contingent. I think that brought out the 'mothering instinct' in some of the waitresses. After the meal we were conducted round the Trophy Room and then onto the pitch. There were plenty of photo opportunities and the enjoyment of it all was plain to see.

Before leaving Ibrox the visitors were given a huge box of Rangers Football Club chocolates. (The kind you get in the corporate hospitality areas, all individually wrapped and with the Rangers crest.) They were also given an equally large box of packets of Rangers' mints and a metal lapel badge with the club's crest. There were free club matches and each visitor received a full colour souvenir book.

This made us late for the next stage, a visit to Parkhead so we telephoned ahead to inform them of our late arrival. When we arrived at Parkhead we were refused entry. Nothing could convince the young man on the front door to let us in. We were late, management had arrived (?) and he was instructed not to let us in. There was no way we could persuade him to let us in so we started to explain this via the interpreter to the Russians and the Poles. Needless to say they were very disappointed and unimpressed!! However someone within Parkhead must have realised just what a PR gaff this was and we were eventually allowed into the trophy room. We were then led to the main stand area but not allowed on to the pitch. There was no tour and no souvenirs.

Two members from the Scottish branch hosted the trip to Stirling and I know they had a very enjoyable day too.

On Tuesday evening the Trident Club was the host for a party to which all boats were invited. There was more than a little concern about how the Russians and the Poles would

FS *Saphir* entering the Clyde submarine base.

Alongside at Faslane.

Alongside at Faslane, seventeen submarines from eleven nations.

get on. However, the worry was unnecessary. Like submariners all over the world, whatever their nationality, once they get a few pints of free beer inside them, it's PARTY TIME!! So a great night was had by all in the junior rate's mess. Not so in the ward room where it is *alleged* that a wee boxing match developed between Russians and Poles. Similarly there is no proof that someone made a serious attempt to change the ward room colour scheme with a rainbow yawn!!

Unfortunately neither Gracie, Bob nor myself attended any of these evening festivities because we were the guests of the first lieutenant of the Russian boat. We could not believe our luck! Their first lt and several of his fellow officers were giving us a guided tour of a Russian Kilo–class submarine. It was truly amazing when you think of all the years we had been playing cat and mouse with each other and now we were wandering around the very class of boat we 'cut our teeth on'. Nothing was hidden from us, any locked doors were unlocked and their friendship and eagerness to please was obvious. We ended the evening in their ward room knocking a serious hole in their vodka stocks. They have a curious method of social drinking. The glasses of vodka are not sipped or savoured; you get a glass full and… wallop! You throw it down your neck. This style of socialising was new to us but we soon caught on!! As we sat chatting via the interpreter someone (usually their doctor) would shout out 'Toast'. The glasses would be topped up and then 'clinked' in the time-honoured manner, then swallowed. This scene repeated itself with alarming regularity and eventually they 'toasted' our queen. We felt that we should reciprocate but were uncertain whom they had as equivalent in rank to our queen. Gracie had the idea and suggested 'Mr. Putin'. There was an embarrassing silence for a moment and a few nervous glances were exchange by our Russian hosts. Clearly we had 'cocked-up'. 'No, no, no,' they said, 'We toast Mother Russia, *She* will always be there for us'. So having developed Anglo-Russian relations to a height never previously reached we knew it was time to go when their captain SM informed us that the first lt. was 'tired'. We all agreed to meet the next night and we would take them to the senior rate's mess in *Neptune*.

Wednesday was the day that Helensburgh Rugby Club hosted a football match and a barbeque. The football was between the Royal Navy and the rest of the world. The RN won but the score varied, depending on who you ask. The game was played in the best spirit and everyone thoroughly enjoyed themselves. Particularly the Norwegian streaker who earned himself nearly £500 in bets by appearing from the surrounding trees, proudly naked and ran all over the pitch pausing only to hug and wrestle to the ground one of the players!! This, as you can guess, was a very amusing interlude. Loud cheers from his shipmates encouraged the streaker! Unknown to him, as he was entertaining the crowd with his antics and very proud display, one of his colleagues crept into the woods and hid his clothes! Imagine his shock when he finally decided to leave the field! However, he eventually found them and re-appeared soon after, fully dressed. The Spanish crew cooked the barbeque and that too was enjoyable.

On Wednesday evening our guests from the Russian boat arrived and we had a very enjoyable evening in the senior rate's mess. It is quite obvious that the Russian crew were intent on being friendly and they came across as very charming people. They asked if we had ever been to Russia and I told them, yes but not officially! They had a good laugh at that and pointed out that this was not their first visit here either!!

Thursday was taken up by a trip to Murrayfield or a trip to Argyll and Bute beauty spots! Once again everyone who took part enjoyed these.

Friday, of course is what it was all about! The Quarry car park has never looked more splendid with its white marquee and grandstand seats.

Each of the eighteen boats had a platoon on parade but only the Russians were applauded as they marched on to their allotted spot! We, the Association, were mustered at the side of the parade ground next to our standards (about half a dozen)

When all the dignitaries and families had taken their seats and everyone had 'fallen in' including the guard, a police car appeared, drove slowly round the car park and disappeared. What was that all about? Any way it amused everyone as we waited for HRH Princess Anne the Princess Royal to arrive.

She did arrive and graciously inspected our guard and colours. The guard, made up mainly of very young 'sailors' was very, very good. They excelled at the march past as did the Russians who 'goose-stepped' past HRH with splendid pomp. The Americans looked as if they were out for a stroll and were waiting for Glen Miller to flash up. It seems surprising that such a large submarine had no ironing facilities!

When everyone else had left the parade the Princess Royal then came over to the Association platoon and spoke to everyone in the front row, the vast majority of whom were submariners.

Some of the international fleet of submarines at Faslane, 2001.

RFV *Vologda* entering Faslane.

Saturday was spent escorting/shepherding visitors to the various submarines for guided tours. A few drinks and a game of ten pin bowling in the famous Swally Alley was the plan for the evening of Saturday. The bowling alley was a very pleasant surprise to me. I expected to find some kind of half-hearted attempt at a bowling alley but this place is an excellent venue. Well worth a visit some time! And the hot dogs are excellent too – and big!! Taste the shape of those rascals!

Sunday started with a service in the packed church, which was attended by a great many senior officers, FOSM, FOSNNI, the captain SM1, etc. Unfortunately, just as we were all ambling towards the church the bandit alarm went off. A false alarm! It seems that the Russian trot sentry, feeling bored and no doubt a wee bit home sick, was idly fiddling

and accidentally set it off. I believe he was impressed by the speed of response of our brave Green Berets, a great many of whom descended on him from all sides.

This was followed by an open-air service at the main mast, again attended by all the *'High Command'*

After a quick pint in the mess it was time to muster the Polish crew and head for the Polish club in Glasgow. A full coach plus a mini bus were soon on their way.

When we all arrived at the club the crew who were all wearing uniform fell in outside the main entrance where the consular general from the embassy gave a welcoming speech and asked the submarine captain to lay a wreath in memory of all Poles killed by the 'Russian oppressors'. Now I don't speak Polish but that phrase cropped up more than a couple of times in his welcome! Before we could say 'Gosh' the whole crew plus the hosts at the club were singing their national anthem. Very melodic. We would find as the day wore on that bursting into song was something they did without much encouragement at all.

Once inside the club a seemingly endless series of speeches and presentations took place. One memorable moment in a speech was when the club president who was really enjoying the occasion, puffed out his chest, paraphrased the first moon landing and coupled with the Polish emblem, proudly announced to loud applause that... 'The eagle has landed in Glasgow'. This was well received although by this time, most of the young sailors were desperate to get stuck into the free drink!

Part of the presentation was the gift of a club tie to Dave Lutwyche our branch chairman and Charlie Nicol representing the Helensburgh branch of the RBLS in appreciation of their efforts in organising the event. Bob Wishart was also presented with a club tie. Finally the drinking could begin and of course the eating of the huge buffet, laid on by the club. After much drinking, eating and spontaneous communal singing we finally returned to the base. It is worth mentioning that there is, apparently, one delicate vodka flavoured with leaves that have matured in bison crap.

I would like to mention that the chairman of the Polish Naval Club expressed to me his wish for a longer lasting association with our branch. That will be done.

The 'enemy' within, Faslane, 2001. A kilo-class attack sub.

A SUBMARINER'S PRAYER

O Father hear our Prayer to Thee,
From your humble servants, beneath the sea,
In the depths of oceans as oft we stray,
So far from Night, so far from Day;
We would ask your guiding light to glow,
To make our journey safe below,
Please oft times grant us patient mind,
Then ere the darkness won't us blind;
We seek thy protection from the deep,
And grant us peace when ere we sleep,
Of our homes and loved ones far away,
We ask you care for them each day;
Until we surface once again,
To drink the air and feel the rain,
We ask your guiding hand to show,
A safe progression sure and slow;
Dear Lord, please hear our Prayer to Thee,
From your humble servants, beneath the sea.

AMEN.

As the week drew to a close the visiting boats left, one by one. However there was one memorable event worthy of mention. The boats were waived off by various senior officers one of whom was Pat Walker, the captain SM1.

As the captain SM1 it was his duty to wave farewell to the visiting boats and he thought that as this was Scotland, bagpipes might be a nice touch.

When the Polish boat was getting ready to leave, he and his piper went to the berth. He commented on the smartness of the casing party who looked splendid in their uniform and as the last line was cast off he turned to give the 'nod' to the piper. When he turned back to salute the departing boat he found the entire casing party and everyone on the bridge including their skipper standing smartly to attention wearing the now infamous 'See you Jimmy' bunnets. (Tartan tammy and long straggly ginger hair)

So much for a solemn moment and a sad farewell!! The piper couldn't play for laughing.

On Monday the boats started to leave for home and so did we.

It was, I feel, an excellent week and I know I speak for the three of us when I say that we enjoyed every minute of it. The Russians even asked us to go over for their Centennial Celebrations in 2006!

At first glance it may look like all we did was piss-up for a week and certainly we did plenty of that but there was a lot of hard work done during the days. We attended the daily meetings of the organising body each morning in Bellmore House at half past eight in the morning. This is where Commander Nick Knox reigned supreme over a large office crowded with young officers. It was quite apparent that the Navy had opened a brand new box of sub-lieutenants for this event. Unfortunately that isn't really what Nick needed. He needed someone who would get out there and do it! Many times I overheard young *subbies* say things like '…that can't be done, sir' or 'I don't think that's possible, sir'. Now, saying that sort of thing to a commander during moments of deep emotional stress is not to be advised. These were young men learning phrases I'm sure they didn't hear very often at home! Oh dear, why should Britain tremble?

Sometimes it did look a bit disorganised and often we didn't know from one moment to the next just what we would be doing. We were even driving mini buses collecting officers and crews from hotels in Glasgow!

The three of us did feel the need for a break by the Monday and I have decided that I'm going to let someone else do it all at the next Centennial Celebration in 2101!

Boats in Faslane for the Centennial Celebrations were:

USS *Tennessee*	America
FS *Saphir*	France
RFV *Vologda*	Russia
HNLMS *Bruinns*	Holland
ORP *Orzel*	Poland
NRP *Delfim*	Portugal
SPS *Tramontata*	Spain
HSWMS *Belos111*	Sweden
HSWMS *Gotland*	Sweden
HNOMS *Svenner*	Norway
FGS U24	*Germany*
FGS U28	*Germany*
HMS/M *Victorious*	UK
HMS/M *Splendid*	UK
HMS/M *Superb*	UK
HMS/M *Sovereign*	UK
HMS/M *Vanguard*	UK

★ ★ ★

SCENE: Nuclear S/M alongside American ship…

S/M: D'yer hear there, finished with main engines and steering fallout harbour stations below, fallout special sea dutymen.

Leave: Leave to the non-duty part of the watch, those men not required for duty check with heads of departments before proceeding ashore …. You are reminded the submarine is under sailing orders …

American ship: Now Hear This, Now Hear This …

Liberty guys to glamourise… all you sailors with bright clean collars and shiny dollars muster at the after smoke stack ….

The Liberty Boat is now afloat …

Tonight's movie will be *The Sands of Iwo Jima* …

seven

The Submariners' Bond

Ken Collins

Submariners' Bond

Many men have served, and are still serving in British submarines. They are all professional men who learn to coexist within the confines of an enclosed hull.

They learn tolerance and trust. Tolerance of each other's human failings and trust in each other, on whom each one's life depends.

Many relationships are made, some closer than others, but all bonded by the special *esprit de corps* which is peculiar to the submariner. The comradeship built on such an existence extends to the families and friends of these submariners and it is of such strength, that it will last forever.

As submariners come to the end of their careers in the Royal Navy and leave to seek their fortune in the totally alien world of 'civvy street', they become separated, town from town, country from country, but their friendships remain as close as ever.

It is with extreme pleasure and no little emotion that when such old and close friends meet again, the time lapses since they last met and the distance that has been between them, fades into insignificance.

An association has been formed to promote the retention of that friendship between submariners both serving and retired from service. That association provides a vehicle to keep track of friends and shipmates no matter how far away they may be and is a catalyst for all friendships to continue and become even stronger.

Formerly the Submarine Old Comrades Association, the newly named Submariners Association is not a collection of venerable veterans of submarine wars but an association of true friendship borne of the submarine service and extended for eternity.

Some may feel that the submariner is a strange breed of man with a somewhat warped outlook on life and a weird sense of humour. The submariner, justifiably, believes he is unique. The capability for man to live in such close proximity to his fellow man naturally extends itself to the families and friends of the submariner. The wives, girlfriends, parents and

Holland 2 alongside HMS *Hazard*

HMS *Valiant*, Britain's first 'home grown' nuclear submarine.

HMS *Conqueror* returning to Faslane after the Falklands War.

siblings are able to look forward to the sometimes ritual demonstrations of friendship.

There are the occasionally sad meetings, to bid goodbye to an old friend as they depart on their last patrol and the memorial parades and meetings held to remember their passing. And there are social gatherings where many old friendships are reinforced and new ones are born. The Submariners Association is that special forum where true friends can continue the unique *esprit de corps* of the submarine service through the rest of their lives.

V-class submarine.

HMS *Resolution*.

A Polaris submarine in the floating dock (AFD 60) at Faslane.

Launch of a trident missile.

HMS *Repulse*.

HMS *Churchill.*

Epilogue

The case for the
defence rests

Need I say more?

At the outset, the publisher asked me to explain why I referred to the submariner as 'the thinking man's matelot'. The submariner is undoubtedly a unique and remarkable individual. Part sailor, part warrior, a true sea-going romantic fearlessly following in the footsteps of Drake or Raleigh. This essential quality is best illustrated by a story I was privileged to overhear a few years ago. Two lads were discussing the film *Topgun*.

'Do you remember the bit where Tom Cruise slept with Kelly McGuiness and left a paper aeroplane on her pillow when he left in the morning?'

'Oh aye, but have you tried knocking a T-boat up out of a lump of A4!

There are a million stories and when the last one's told there'll be a million more.

Submariner humour is not a laughing matter. It is a result of his lifestyle and his method of dealing with life's tribulations. It should be stressed that if swanning around on the surface of the world's oceans was such a good idea, mre fish would do it.

I hope you've enjoyed the book; for submariners, I hope it has stirred a few memories. These memories and the pictures that support them are now the 'Keepers of the Past' and as such, we have some 'co-operate' responsibility to look after them and keep them alive. For those people who suffer the chronic disadvantage of not being a submariner, there's still time.

The case for the defence rests.

Other titles published by Tempus

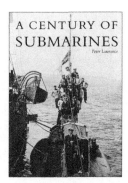

A Century of Submarines
PETER LAWRENCE

The first submarines to be commissioned by the British Admiralty were five 'Holland' class boats in 1900. Arriving in 1901, they heralded a new age of naval warfare. The British submarine service took a long time to grow, however, due to naval rivalries and hierarchies and an institutional misinterpretation of submarine tactics and strategy. Complemented by nearly 200 illustrations, Peter Lawrence's knowledgeable and passionate account of submarine history will appeal to those interested in the tactics and politics of war as well as those with a more specialist interest in the submarine.

0 7524 1755 X

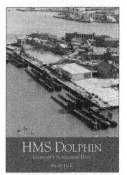

HMS Dolphin Gosport's Submarine Base
KEITH HALL

In the latter half of the nineteenth century the Gosport side of Portsmouth harbour was   developed as a fortified port. Fort Blockhouse, originally established in 1495, was updated and became the home of the Royal Engineers' Submarine Mining School in 1873. In *HMS Dolphin*, Keith Hall charts the history of the base and the HMS Dolphin fleet – a narrative complemented by over 200 illustrations.

0 7524 2113 1

Damned Un-English Machines
A History of Barrow-Built Submarines
JACK HOOL AND KEITH NUTTER

The shipbuilding works at Barrow-in-Furness has been the hub of the Royal Navy's submarine-building programme for more than a century. This comprehensive treatment of the subject, including references to commercial 'mini-subs', First and Second World War German submarines and the reactivation of the Canadian Upholder Class, provides an exceptional narrative that will become a valuable reference in the future.

0 7524 2781 4

Supermarine
DR NORMAN BARFIELD

Supermarine was founded in 1913 on the Woolston shore of the River Itchen at Southampton by Noel Pemberton Billing, with the intention to 'build boats that fly rather than aeroplanes that float'. In the post-war jet age, Supermarine produced three generations of jet fighters – the 'Attacker', the 'Swift' and the 'Scimitar', the Royal Navy's first swept-wing jet aircraft. This collection of over 200 photographs portrays one of the most creative chapters in British aeronautical history.

0 7524 0605 1

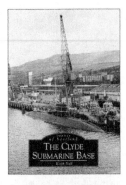

The Clyde Submarine Base
KEITH HALL

The Clyde Submarine Base was officially commissioned in 1967. The Faslane site had originally been used as a military port during the Second World War, and was built and manned by the army. This book traces the development of the submarine base in unsurpassed pictorial detail, from its initial use by the army in 1996, when the base became HM Naval Base Clyde. Sure to be of interest to sub enthusiasts.

0 7524 1657 X

Dark Seas Above HM Submarine Taurus
JOHN FREDERICK GIBSON

This is the story of war at sea as seen by a young submarine officer. In telling it, the author draws a vivid picture of the 'daily round and common tasks' of life in submarines, illuminated from time to time by the highlights of quick and decisive action, attack and counter-attack. This book will help, hopefully, to show just what debt of gratitude Britain and her Allies owe to all submariners of the nations that helped to destroy Hitler's ambitions.

0 7524 2018 6

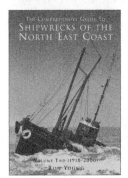

Shipwrecks of the North East Coast Volume Two (1918–2000)
RON YOUNG

In this second volume, from the last years of the Second World War, to the end of the twentieth century, Ron Young charts the history of the ships, boats, submarines and their crews, that were lost along the north–east coast from Berwick-on-Tweed to Whitby, and the brave lifeboat crews that went to their aid, whatever the danger to themselves. This comprehensive guide is an absorbing companion volume to Shipwrecks of the North East Coast – Volume One (1740 – 1917)

0 7524 1750 9

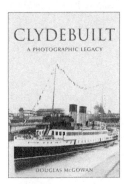

Clydebuilt A Photographic Legacy
DOUGLAS MCGOWAN

The River Clyde holds a special fascination for many. Its interesting mix of industrial and urban landscape contrasting with its weathered mountain grandeur has been an enduring joy for the past two hundred years. The Clyde has been home to many a skilled engineer and naval architect from Robert Napier to William Denny and has seen some of the finest shipbuilding in the world. Here, Douglas McGowan, a lifelong Clyde shipping enthusiast, brings together his favourite selection of Clydebuilt ships, using many fascinating and previously unpublished images.

0-7524-3228-1

If you are interested in purchasing other books published by Tempus, or in case you have difficulty finding any Tempus books in your local bookshop, you can also place orders directly through our website
www.tempus-publishing.com